Scotland's Local Food Revolution

Mike Small

ARGYLL ✠ PUBLISHING

© Mike Small 2013

Argyll Publishing
Glendaruel
Argyll PA22 3AE

www.argyllpublishing.co.uk
www.centreforconfidence.co.uk
www.postcardsfromscotland.co.uk
www.fifediet.co.uk

British Library Cataloguing-in-Publication Data.

A catalogue record for this book is available from the British Library.

ISBN 978 1 908931 26 9

Printing
Martins the Printers, Berwick upon Tweed

CONTENTS

Acknowledgements   6

Introduction   7

One   Globalised food   13

Two   Horses for courses   37

Three   Big Shopping   51

Four   Living within limits   65

Five   Community through food   75

Six   Scottish perspectives   89

Seven   Scotland's local food revolution   107

Eight   What you can do   118

References   121

Notes   123

Acknowledgements

Many thanks to all of my colleagues and friends at the Fife Diet, who are all a source of huge inspiration: Elly Kinross, Meg Elphee, Fergus Walker, Mags Hall, Teresa Martinez, and to Wendy Gudmundsson for unstinting support in the last five years. Thanks also to Justin Kenrick for ideas and hope, to Colin Lindsay for much needed rigour and endless good cheer (and bread). Thanks to Joanna Blythman for critical thinking (a rare commodity) and to Iain Anderson, Tara O Leary, Ingrid Schebesch, and Serge Marti.

But most of all special thanks to my wife Karen for ongoing support and patience and to my three sons Sorley, Alex and Calum for whom I hope for a better future.

Introduction

This book is about our climate crisis and how it's tied to our bloated consumer culture and our dysfunctional food system. It's about how our society has become dominated by values not of most people's making and how the resultant exploitation is leading us into socio-ecological disaster. It's about how we are living through an 'intentional epidemic' of obesity and how the food industry is at odds with the public interest, a reality recently exposed by the horsemeat scandal.

This may sound like grim reading but this is a profoundly hopeful book. Of course, it shows that our food system is fundamentally wrong but at its core is the realisation that there's something we can do about it. Indeed much of this book is about the growing movement that's creating a 'restorative practice' that could help nurture community, as well as providing affordable and nourishing food for everyone. It outlines the ideas and motivations that have led many thousands of people in Scotland to turn away from industrialised food and its accompanying ill-health.

Most of us live our lives hoping, expecting or dreaming that some external agency will solve our environmental problems. We hope that divine intervention or even the free market will help out. Surely a benign government will step in and enact environmental laws that will make things better? Maybe we'll shop our way to a better future. Maybe someone will 'invent' a solution to our problems. After all, technology has helped us out in the past.

There's a whole stratum of 'greens' who think like this. These 'bright greens', as they're called, believe that technology and other ingenious solutions will allow us to 'fix' the environment without altering our relationship with nature or the fundamental problems which gave rise to the environmental crisis in the first place. Not only is this implausible, technology itself is increasingly at the root of the problem leading to a proliferation of gadgets, processes and techniques that use more, not less, energy.

In looking at how we can start to solve the problems of our dysfunctional food system we need to learn lessons from the wider ecology movement. There's a growing realisation that previous efforts to tackle environmental degradation and the problem of runaway climate change are based on old ways of thinking and acting. As with individuals, these outdated modes of thought are mostly about persuading some other agency to act on our behalf. This is why charities and campaign groups have devoted considerable time and resources to lobbying governments, and petitioning others to enact legislation. But this approach is the failed basis of much, if not most, environmental 'strategy' today. The environmental dreams of shifting a capitalist economy so that businesses curb or moderate their rapacious and exploitative practices have been undermined at every turn.

Ironically hope for real action and change has been undermined in part because businesses have embraced environmentalists' concerns so enthusiastically. 'Corporate capture' and 'greenwash' are the terms used to describe this phenomenon. For example, supermarkets, whose business practices generate huge environmental problems, use glossy adverts to tout their green credentials whilst making small, meaningless changes.

Meanwhile on almost any measure you choose from carbon emissions, to preventing soil degradation, to creating a legal framework to turn this momentum of destruction around this approach to change has failed. And failed spectacularly. Indeed governments are showing that they are largely incapable of making a difference at both the national and international level. In the last few years the Scottish Government has proved incapable of curbing the growth of plastic bags, never mind tackling climate change. When we examine any sign of apparent success what we'll often find is that it's little more than an amelioration of the problem and nothing like a long-term cure.

The Fife Diet, and much of the local food revolution that has swept Scotland in the past five years, has been driven by the realisation that few if any of these external agencies are motivated or equipped to act. *It is up to us to change our behaviour and way of being and we must do so on an unprecedented grand scale*. We must be the change. We must heed the visionary Russian thinker Peter Kropotkin's injunction: 'Act for yourself'.

There's a recurrent phrase that encapsulates this growing

realisation of what the change involves: 'I kept wondering why somebody didn't do something. Then I realised, I was somebody.'

By creating food networks and systems based on a different set of values than the ones we are continually urged to adopt, we can begin to establish routes to a low-carbon society founded on a genuinely sustainable, resilient economy. This new food system will be capable of nourishing both people and places.

This change is essential given the relationship between carbon and food. Previous estimates by the Food Climate Research Network and others suggested that the food chain accounts for around 20% of the UK's greenhouse gas emissions. However, new research in 2010 found that, once food related land use change impacts were included in the calculation, food's contribution to greenhouse gases rises to 30% of the UK total.[1]

But it's actually worse than that. If we take into account land appropriated abroad to satisfy our demand for out of season fruit and vegetables – strawberries from Morocco or green beans grown in Kenya, for example – then food contributes even more to the UK's carbon footprint or 'foodprint' as it should perhaps be called.

Thousands of people in Scotland are already convinced of the need to take action and are altering their own relationship with food. However, the realities of austerity and the conservatism that can evoke, plus the rampant denial about the climate crisis are obstacles to real change.

George Monbiot, writing about Cormac McCarthy's dystopian fiction *The Road*, wondered: 'Are we already shutting our minds to the consequences of climate change?' He writes:

> The stone drops into the pond and a second later it is smooth again. You will turn the page and carry on with your life. Last week we learnt that climate change could eliminate half the world's species; that 25 primate species are already slipping into extinction; that biological repositories of carbon are beginning to release it, decades ahead of schedule. But everyone is watching and waiting for everyone else to move. The unspoken universal thought is this: if it were really so serious, surely someone would do something? [2]

What is on our side, however, is how connected we now are. We now have the communication tools to create waves of change and establish 'network enabled collaboration'. As we shall see, this allows us to act not as solitary dispossessed and powerless individuals but as effective communities, co-ordinated regions and citizen-led urban activists.

'The traditional Scottish diet was once wholesome and hearty. . . [but] it's hardly surprising that Scottish cooking traditions, like many other aspects of Scottish culture, were not only ignored but ridiculed.'

'It's clear that the industrialised food system has massive productive capacity and is hugely rewarding and profitable for companies and owners. . . But it's quite clear that its purpose isn't to provide nutritious food or a steady income for farmers. It's simply about making money and creating shareholder value.'

CHAPTER ONE

Globalised food

We may be the first species to 'choose' a diet that is
killing us and destroying our planet.
Frances Moore Lappé

The Romans used to import oysters from the Thames to
Rome. They did so because they could. They had the trading
routes, the cultural extravagance, and obviously the desire
to eat the best oysters they had ever tasted. It was a display of
opulence and empire.

In contemporary times we transport our seafood to
Thailand to be washed and then returned to us in a tin. We
do this because it's cheap. We accept the long distance
transportation of food because we don't really think about
it. Indeed we are encouraged not to think about where our
food comes from or goes to, and largely speaking, we comply.

Occasionally reality intervenes and disturbs our eating. This
is what happened in the first few months of 2013 when we
discovered that horsemeat from various European countries
was cropping up in all sorts of meat products sold in the UK.

Given the Romans' penchant for oysters from the banks of
the Thames, or the importation of spices from the Orient

✦

even in the Middle Ages, it's clear that there has always been a level of trade, exchange, importation and engagement with food from far-off places. However, we have now reached a level of globalised food that is devastatingly polluting, culturally damaging and psychologically disorientating.

Most of us in the West have grown up with what passes as a 'food culture' but which is really little more than a guided and prescriptive consumer experience that hovers above nature and takes little or no interest in season, place, geography or even taste. Food is no more than a commodity. Animals are products. Globalised food is now the norm. What results is not a celebration of different cultures but a fusion – or guddle – where nothing is authentic or of real value.

For the generation that lived through rationing in the Second World War, or experienced the dull Scottish diet of the 1960s and 70s, exotic imports were a godsend. People's appetites were whetted by a whole range of factors: exposure to the mass media, particularly American shows which often featured food which was dramatically different from what was available at home; advertising; the proliferation of new Indian and Chinese restaurants as a result of the growing immigrant population; and the rise of supermarkets and the explosion of what was now available in the shops. People also started to travel abroad for their holidays and this too increased their interest in Italian, Spanish and French cuisine.

However, what began as a helpful expansion of people's interest in different types of food soon became a runaway train of expectations and a food culture where you expect to have anything, anytime, from anywhere. What started as an adventure and a sampling of fare from around the world became little more than a fusion-mush of inauthentic dishes and a cliché of world cuisines.

Inevitably this also meant that our own food culture was waylaid. The traditional Scottish diet was once wholesome and hearty. But the accent was on plain fare. Food was more about keeping body and soul together and giving people the energy to work hard and survive the cold weather rather than on taste, savouring or the joys of eating. Poor standards of cooking were also all too common but perhaps understand-able in a country with inadequate housing stock and considerable poverty. So it's hardly surprising that Scottish cooking traditions, like many other aspects of Scottish culture, were not only ignored but ridiculed. Foreigners may not have been that positive about Scottish cuisine but often the worst criticisms were made by Scots themselves. For example, writing in the mid 1950s Moray McLaren maintained:

> Since the Industrial Revolution and the creation of the large cities . . . the average Scot hardly cares what he eats at all. Or if he is selective it is only to dislike and reject any refined or delicate form of cooking. The food offered in the average public, eating place in Scotland is lamentable. It is dull, overcooked, tasteless and presented completely without imagination. [3]

Nonetheless McLaren recognises how 'superb good Scottish food' can be 'if cooked and presented in the traditional way.'

Given that Scottish cooking was for many boring and unim-aginative, it's hardly surprising that Scots have particularly fallen in love with globalised food and lost perspective on what's available locally. Scotland is the largest exporter of soft fruit in Europe yet people still look at you incredulous if you say you eat local food in Scotland. 'But what fruit do you eat?' is still a regular outraged response. Just as people can't imagine not eating meat with almost every meal, many people can't imagine going a day without tropical fruit, at any time of the year. Undoubtedly we've got a taste for it but we are only beginning to wake up to the issues that a trans-national supra-natural food system causes.

The madness of globalised food

We now fly, ship and truck food around the world and pretend there is no environmental cost. We do this to sustain the illusion that seasons (and nature) don't exist and to maintain the myth of limitless consumer choices. The trucking of food rose by 50% and air-freighting more than doubled between 1978 and 2002.[4] Flying accounts for only 1% of UK food miles, but generates 10% of food transport CO2 emissions. Shipping is also a major problem. The amount of sulphur oxide pollution that comes from the 15 largest ships equals the combined amount from all the cars in the world. When we talk about 'food miles' we are not just talking about air freight we are talking about the whole journey between gate and plate including the endless shuttling between home and the giant out of town shopping malls we call supermarkets.

A snapshot of the madness which is globalised food comes from the Green MP Caroline Lucas who produced the following information on UK food imports and exports. It is so nonsensical that it has produced audible gasps when I've presented it at some public talks:

• Pork – exports 195,000 tonnes / imports 240,000 tonnes

- Lamb – exports 102,000 tonnes / imports 47,000 tonnes

- Butter – exports 49,000 tonnes / imports 47,000 tonnes

- Poultry – exports 170,000 tonnes / imports 363,000 tonnes

- Fresh Milk – exports 119,000 tonnes / imports 114,000 tonnes

- Live Pigs – exports 110,000 pigs / imports 200,000 pigs [5]

Who would have invented such a system? What are the refrigeration costs? The fuel costs? What is the moral justification for transporting live animals unnecessarily? How did we get here? What can we do?

But we have an alternative, and increasingly we're turning to it. One aspect of the current food system – the processed meat industry – has unwittingly turned a spotlight not only on the globalised nature of the food we eat but also on its unsavoury, if not actually corrupt, practices. We're now in a period of uncertain but rapid change.

As a result of the horsemeat scandal six out of ten consumers changed their shopping habits. Consumer trust in the meat industry was cut by a quarter and confidence in supermarket food has dropped through the floor. People felt shocked. The public expected someone to be looking out for their well-being and was surprised to find that nobody really cared much. [6]

Food miles – the system by which food is transported around the world as part of a globalised food culture – is often seen primarily as an ecological issue. This means that the focus is on needless and endless emissions. But in fact it's also an issue of transparency, accountability and ultimately, democracy. Thankfully it is now firmly on our agenda for where food comes from has become a massive political and consumer issue. We're beginning to wake up to some basic shocking facts: we don't know what's in our food; we can't understand the process it goes through to get to us; no one seems responsible for this; and nobody really cares.

Provenance – where your food comes from – has also dramatically changed from being a cheffy, foody issue to one of national public interest. Indeed what happened in the UK in the first few months of 2013 has blown open the problems of a food system based on anonymous, deregulated, out-sourced relationships. At the heart of this swirling pigsty of cheap low quality processed food is the reality of industrial meat production. It may be difficult to swallow but this is what we blithely call 'convenience' food.

The horsemeat crisis, which we'll examine more fully in the next chapter, is more about globalised food than it is about meat type. As food writer Felicity Lawrence has noted:

> The story of how horsemeat ended up inside hundreds of millions of cheap burgers and beef ready meals has opened a window on the hidden, unsavoury food world, in which live animals are transported vast distances across borders for slaughter, before being stripped down to constituent parts to be shipped back again in blocks of frozen offcuts that may be stored for months on end before being ground down to unrecognisable ingredients in our everyday meals.[7]

The current meat 'scandal' has blown open the inherent crisis at the heart of food distribution networks. Key to this atrocity is the easy and cheap movement of food about the planet till it becomes little more than an anonymous mass: meat as commodity for a passive and unknowing consumer.

It's important not to think of this as 'crisis'. This *is* the system. It is not an aberration. As food writer Joanna Blythman points out:

> This globalised buying system not only encourages fraud and adulteration but also presents opportunities for it. Who can tell if they're eating beef, horse, donkey, or even dog, when it's reconstituted with water, fillers and additives and looking plausible, in a supermarket-endorsed box? [8]

Sustainable food

The only credible response to this in Scotland, as elsewhere, is to create a revolution in food production, with radically shortened supply chains, more direct relationships between producers and consumers and an entirely different sense of food geography. The very definition of 'consumer' and 'producer' has been distorted and needs to be further changed so that the production is taken out of the hands of a few and distributed amongst many.

The current food system can only work if people don't think about the food they eat and don't question where it comes from. It's an absurd system which depends on a complacent consumer, and a deep-seated quietism that neither knows nor cares about the origins of foodstuffs.

Re-localising is only part of the answer to our complex set of problems. There is nothing necessarily ideal about a 'local food system'. Any change must pass a number of other key tests to be sustainable. It must be based on inputs that are part of a closed loop system. It must be based on a healthy soil, rich in nutrients. It must be based on 'food sovereignty' whereby people have some element of control over what they eat and how it's grown, and it must have a sense of respect for producers and consumers – a respect which is conspicuously absent in the current set-up. So re-localisation is only part of the diagnosis in healing a sick system, but it is a crucial step.

Crucially a *local food system* is one that is traceable, transparent and accountable. Localism is inadequate in itself – you can have some terrible food produced in terrible conditions 'locally' – and there would be nothing good about that. Nonetheless re-configuring the global to the local is the *sine qua non* of sustainability.

We must begin to re-localise our food chain, and that means breaking the supermarkets' vice-like grip on it as they are key players in the globalisation of food. If we continue to rely on faceless people in faraway places to feed us, we cannot hope to trace the provenance of what's on our plates, or be assured of its wholesomeness. In the future, horsemeat may be the least of our problems.

As the local food revolution gathers strength the number of people making connections and creating a critical culture is increasing not just in size but also in insight and clarity. The current system only works if people are passive consumers whose judgement is simply channelled into discriminating between largely identical brands. We now have, for the first time, a large number of people who are critically aware of the problems in food, agriculture, health, well-being and ecology. For a food culture that has had, until very recently, only one single over-riding metric – 'Is it very cheap?' – this is a new phenomenon.

People have begun to question everything from the production process their food goes through, to the pesticides, insecticides and herbicides used in that production. They are also questioning how their food is cooked and the amount of waste it produces. The exploitation inherent in the system and its ethics, whether this is how *foie gras* is produced or the use of slave gangs, are also under scrutiny. People are also beginning to question why we are seeing surges in wheat and dairy allergies; why seeds need to be patented; why kids are getting fat before they're ten; why we need to import bottled water into Scotland; how we've affected bee colonies . . . and everything in between.

It's not difficult to see why all of this is now in the front of people's minds. Indeed as the 'local food revolution' gathers strength a more pertinent question is why it hasn't got even more vigour and anger?

How did we get here?

In the last few years many unsavoury aspects of the food system have been exposed – not just Salmonella and BSE but also Foot and Mouth, Avian Flu (H5N1) and the new disease called Blue Tongue. This is all on top of the regular exposure of the horrors not only of battery egg production but also battery farming.

It's clear that the industrialised food system has massive productive capacity and is hugely rewarding and profitable for companies and owners. But its core recurring weakness is that it's not *for* people. It's quite clear that its purpose isn't to provide nutritious food or a steady income for farmers. It's simply about making money and creating shareholder value.

The dangers of industrialised food, and its dedication to profit, are most evident if we look at three catastrophic food related crises: BSE, H5N1 and the horsemeat scandal.

In 1986 'mad cow disease' or BSE was first identified in cattle. Ten years later the then Conservative Government announced that the disease had jumped the species barrier to humans. The Government admitted that the strange new brain disease vCJD was probably linked to BSE and that it was likely that victims had caught the disease by eating meat from BSE infected cattle.

A special BSE Inquiry was set up in 1998 to investigate the public health scandal. The Phillips report on the Government's handling of the BSE crisis was published on 26 October 2000. It concluded that the main cause of the disease was the feeding of MBM (meat and bone meal) to previously uninfected cattle. Cattle are normally herbivores, so the feeding of MBM meant that they were being fed the remains of other cattle. It's not difficult for any untrained person to understand that if you feed MBM to uninfected cattle this allows the disease to spread more rapidly. The infectious agent involved in BSE is unusual because it remains active even at high temperatures. The rendering process (by which animal remains are made into useful byproducts) involves heating.

However in Britain the temperatures reached during rendering had been reduced, no doubt to save money. This meant that the infectious agent remained active and therefore capable of spreading more rapidly.

The first UK death from the horrific, long-incubating vCJD – that of 19-year-old Stephen Churchill – occurred in 1995. The bombshell of a possible link to BSE was announced by the Government in March the following year. By that time the peak of BSE infection in cattle had passed. We probably don't know how many animals were culled. But we do know that cattle deaths from BSE in England, Scotland and Wales, numbered 36,680 in 1992 and 34,370 in 1993. Millions of other cows were destroyed because they were too old to go into human or animal food.

The human death toll from vCJD in the UK is contested, but we can safely say it was between 100 and 1,000 deaths.

The tragedy of BSE was not the predictable Government cover-up, the inevitable industry propaganda or the devastation of the farming community. The tragedy was that lessons weren't learnt and the food industry forced to make widespread changes. Had the disastrous impacts of these industrial food crises been thought about, and the production relationships that created them challenged, we might have established a set of rigorous tests and regulations to check and control the food we eat.

But that's not what happened as we found out in 2007 when Bird Flu hit Britain. The BSE scandal arose because we were feeding cattle to cattle. Soon we were to discover that not only were poultry producers feeding chickens to chickens but also chicken shit to chickens.

As the famous environmentalist James Bruges has pointed out: 'In the light of the previous BSE crisis, it is scarcely believable that chicken feed is still permitted to include poultry litter (bird faeces), feathers and waste meat.' [9]

The first response to the Bird Flu virus was to blame it on nature. But ultimately investigators found no evidence of H5N1 in wild birds in Britain nor of undisclosed infection in domestic poultry in Britain. The problem was largely confined to Bernard Matthews' Suffolk turkey 'farm' as it was euphemistically called. They had to cull 159,000 turkeys to prevent the H5N1 virus spreading. There was widespread disbelief when they were given £600,000 in compensation for birds slaughtered during the Bird Flu outbreak despite flagrant hygiene lapses at its Suffolk plant. So the industrial system that created the problem was compensated while the natural and small-scale bird keeping was demonised and castigated.

Worse still, broader lessons have not been learned. We are now putting Equidae (horse and horse-related animals) into food consumed by humans.

Change is now inevitable

In response to these sporadic, but regular crises, over the last few years we've seen the start of a local food revolution that could find fruition in a new set of standards, values and expectations in what and how we eat.

This rise in consciousness about food has been building in waves over a number of decades. The striking thing about this local food revolution is how international it is. Ironically, it is influenced by global culture and the best and worst of American food trends.

So what's beginning to happen in Scotland, and will be charted later in this book, hasn't emerged in a vacuum. There's been a growing popular narrative about the problems in our food economy for years and it's now beginning to stretch beyond the confines of the ethical food movement and into the popular imagination. It's worth outlining here a few of the key figures who have led this growth in popular consciousness.

Under the pseudonym Lewis Herber, the American social ecologist Murray Bookchin wrote about food in the early 1950s. Starting in 1952, Bookchin began writing about 'the problem of chemicals in food' for the New York-based journal *Contemporary Issues.* He argued that the use of pesticides, herbicides, and other chemicals in agriculture was having toxic effects on human health. To reduce the need for them, he advocated a marriage of town and country – that is, producing food near where it is to be consumed and sowing, maintaining, and harvesting crops locally. He criticised the use of monocultures and called for crop diversity. He condemned the exhaustion of topsoil and called for crop rotation. He also denounced large-scale, centralised agriculture, which reduced farmers to labourers, and called instead for small-scale farming, in which those who worked the land maintained a valued connection to the natural world.

Shortly after Bookchin published his critique, the more popular, if less political, Rachel Carson wrote her seminal work *Silent Spring* (1962), which warned of the potential devastation of song birds by pesticide contamination in America. Its title was inspired by a poem by John Keats, 'La Belle Dame sans Merci', which contained the lines 'The sedge is wither'd from the lake, And no birds sing.' The book is widely held to be the starting point of the American environmental movement.

In the 1970s the work of people like Frances Moore Lappé was hugely influential in raising awareness of food politics. Her book *Diet for a Small Planet* (1971) was a best-seller and the first major book to critique grain-fed meat production as wasteful and a contributor to global food scarcity.

Throughout her works Lappé has argued that world hunger is caused not by the lack of food but rather by the inability of hungry people to gain access to the world's abundance of food or food-producing resources because they are simply too poor. She has posited that our current 'thin democracy' creates a mal-distribution of power and resources that inevitably creates waste and an artificial scarcity of the essentials for sustainable living.

Lappé argues that what she calls 'living democracy', i.e. not only what we do in the voting booth but through our daily choices of what we buy and how we live, provides a mental and behavioural framework of goods and goodness that is aligned with our basic human nature. She believes that only by 'living democracy' can we effectively solve today's social and environmental crises.

In the UK in the 1990s a massive legal case was brought by burger giant McDonalds against a tiny green group which had published a pamphlet entitled *What's wrong with*

McDonald's: Everything they don't want you to know. The original case lasted ten years, from 1987-1997 making it the longest-running case in English history. The trial became a fantastic protest opportunity for anyone who had an issue with commercialised fast food. If McDonald's won the actual legal battle they lost the war, with Helen Steel and David Morris (often referred to as 'The McLibel Two') gaining huge support and being able to call key McDonald's executives as witnesses.

The pair also had important elements of their accusations substantiated. The judges ruled that it was fair comment to say that McDonald's employees worldwide 'do badly in terms of pay and conditions' and true that 'if one eats enough McDonald's food, one's diet may well become high in fat etc., with the very real risk of heart disease.' They further stated that this last finding 'must have a serious effect on their trading reputation since it goes to the very business in which they are engaged. In our judgment, it must have a greater impact on the respondents' [McDonald's] reputation than any other of the charges that the trial judge had found to be true.' [10]

The McLibel trial was a breakthrough for many people in the UK gaining an insight into corporate power and was seen by many as an iconic moment when 'brandwashing', as it is called, ceased to work. Each of these events and publications chipped away at the public's confidence in Big Food and a critical understanding became more mainstream.

The McLibel trial debate was followed by a series of breakthrough documentaries. First there was *Fast Food Nation: The Dark Side of the All-American Meal* (2003) a book written by Eric Schlosser which was then made into a film with the same name (2006). Then the filmmaker Morgan Spurlock made a documentary called *Super Size Me* (2004) which enlightened a whole new generation about problems in fast food. For thirty days Spurlock only ate McDonald's food and during the period gained more than 24 lbs of weight, increased his body mass by 13%, raised his cholesterol and experienced mood problems and sexual dysfunction. It took him 14 months and a vegan diet to recover. Schlosser later worked with Robert Kenner and Michael Pollan on another documentary called *Food Inc* (2008) which looked at corporate farming in the USA and its harmful effects on the environment, animals and employees.

Parallel to this unfolding cultural analysis was a series of celebrity interventions in the UK. *Jamie's School Dinners* (2005), and *Hugh's Fish Fight* (2012) saw television chefs, Jamie Oliver and Hugh Fearnley-Whittingstall, raise ethical issues and bring them to the public attention in the complete absence of any meaningful action from the UK Government. While there's something almost comical about food policy being determined by television personalities, the reality is that they have raised awareness of wider food issues.

Food volatility – the perfect storm

The food system often looks as if it is seized by forces of inertia and the retail system impregnable, yet key drivers of change are forcing a new reality. As climate chaos beckons and weather systems falter, other factors combine to drive change.

Food prices rose after a summer of wet weather hit harvests in 2012. The global price of wheat rose by 30% during the year. Potato harvests were down by half in some areas. The NFU's Scottish cereal survey indicated wheat yield was down by 18% from 2011, winter barley yield down 7%, spring barley yield down 18% and winter oilseed rape yield down 26%.

Apple growers in England say it was the worst harvest for 12 years and Save the Children report that food price rises and volatility are the 'new normal'. Shoppers are also being affected by higher prices for other crops, with global grain costs hit by American drought and the Russian heatwave. This yo-yoing between flood and drought may be nothing in comparison with the inherent problem of Western culture of knowing how to live and increasingly unable to feed itself properly.

This isn't an exaggeration emanating from what we could call green miserabilism. New research by consumer group Which? found that the average cost of a shopping bill is now £76.83 per week – an increase of £5.66 on the previous year. Their executive director, Richard Lloyd reported:

> Household budgets are under enormous strain and our research has shown rising food prices are a top concern. More people are shopping at discount supermarkets and one in four say they are planning to cut food spending in the next few months. [11]

Waitrose's managing director, Mark Price, stated in January 2013 that current food price increases were 'only the tip of the iceberg'.[12] Some estimate that food prices will rise by at least 4% per annum for the next decade. The UK is particularly susceptible to food increases as Britain currently imports around 40% of what it consumes.

Only three years ago, the UK Government's chief scientific

adviser, Sir John Beddington, warned that the world faced a 'perfect storm' of food, water and energy problems, due to global warming and the rising global population. Elements of that perfect storm are now with us.

Doubters can read a whole range of reports summarising scientific findings or read the study released by Munich Re, the world's largest reinsurance firm, which sees climate change driving increased weather volatility and predicting that those influences will continue in the years ahead. [13]

It's clear we need to change the way we 'do' food. We need to make food part of the solution not a growing part of the problem of climate change.

But this isn't going to be easy as it contradicts some of our fundamental assumptions about food. First, we must stop clinging to the myth that changing weather patterns are going to be good for us in northern Europe. This often shows itself in remarks about how in the future we shall have orchards or vineyards in 'unusual places'. As the realities of globalised food and a fundamentally altered weather system come to the fore I think we'll be hearing a lot less of this type of gallows talk.

Second we also have an inherent notion of 'bounty' or 'plentitude'. It's a modern day sense of entitlement wrapped up in a lovely jumble of pagan and Christian symbolism which is most evident at Thanksgiving. However, nowadays our sense of living from the cornucopia of a fertile land has been transformed into our expectations of harvesting globalised food from the shelves of 24-hour Tescos. Our assumption is that food just gushes out, endlessly. Doesn't it?

Finally, and most importantly, we need to ditch the assumption that food should be cheap. Indeed we must stop thinking that unlimited cheap food is our birthright. Just as we are having to accept that house prices do not continually rise or petrol so cheap and available that we can drive anywhere we like, we need to acknowledge that there is not an abundance of cheap food. We need to understand food and respect where it comes from and treat it as something of real value.

What is to be done?

So what can we do? In response to climate change we have to change our thinking about how we do food and farming from one of mitigation to adaptation. We definitely have to change our model of farming from one of vast mono-crop farms which are heavily dependent on external inputs and highly vulnerable to failure, to more diverse and smaller scale units. Such a change has huge consequences for land ownership, tenancy, planning law and urban agriculture. We'll have to look at how we can create much shorter supply chains using less energy and utilising routes and networks. This new system will be far less vulnerable to failures and shocks than our current and vastly over-extended globalised food system.

We should abandon 'yield' as the sole metric of farming success. Just as the concept of 'growth' has driven Western economies to ruin, yield has made farming completely unsustainable. We need to drastically reduce waste for example by eating 'ugly food' such as misshapen or pitted fruits. We need to stop subsidising biofuels and begin to wrestle the food system back from Big Farming, the multiples and the handful of companies that dominate our broken food system. Diversity, open source farming and food sovereignty are all key.

In Scotland some good work is well under way. In 2007 the Scottish Government published a national discussion paper called 'Choosing the right ingredients'. From this emerged *A Recipe for Success* (2009) – Scotland's first national food and drink policy. It was ground-breaking in trying to develop a 'cross-cutting' policy and putting affordability and local sustainable food at the heart of plans for changing the way we grow and eat our food. It promised a 'holistic approach' when awarding food and catering contracts, the adoption of sustainable food procurement as a corporate objective for all public sector organisations, the extension of free school lunches, and an increase in the uptake of healthy start vouchers for pregnant women and children.

There has been a fantastic focus on food in Scotland in the past few years. The £27 million Climate Challenge Fund has helped over 250 communities reduce their emissions, saving an estimated 700,000 tonnes of CO_2. That's the equivalent of taking 225,000 cars off Scotland's roads. Over half these projects have focused partly or wholly on food sustainability, representing £9 million in funding.

While this is all most welcome we need to work at an entirely higher level. Think of the commitment, research, ambition and investment we've seen in transforming Scottish energy in the last twenty years and you get some idea of what we need to do to transform our food infrastructure.

If we have established the goal of 100% renewable energy and have mobilised considerable resources to make that feasible, how do our efforts in sustainable food look by comparison? They look pretty inadequate.

Food and health

In his foreword to *Recipe for Success*, Richard Lochhead, Cabinet Secretary for Rural Affairs and the Environment, pointed out:

> There is a strange Scottish paradox, despite producing fantastic food and drink we have one of the poorest diet-related health records in the developed world. A host of factors contributes to our poor diet. Whatever the reasons for our dietary habits, our culture must change if we are to prosper as a nation. We should be making our food choices in a more balanced way, taking account of food's healthiness, quality, seasonality and freshness. [14]

So far I have outlined the environmental necessity behind a shift in our approach to food but health is another huge issue. The latest Scottish health statistical review stated that

> Excess consumption of saturated fat, salt and sugar, and low consumption of fruit and vegetables, are all risk factors associated with one or more of heart disease, cancer, hypertension, type 2 diabetes and obesity. [15]

The first book in this series, *AfterNow* by Professor Phil Hanlon and Dr Sandra Carlisle, showed that health in Scotland is poorer than it is in other equivalent countries.

The notion of '5 a day' is now well understood across most of the Scottish population, but the number of people acting on that knowledge is far lower. In fact consumption of fruit and vegetables in Scotland only increased from 3 portions to 3.5 in 2010. This is still 1.5 portions below the 5 a day target. Basically, we're not eating enough fresh food, and overall consumption of healthy foods is significantly lower in the most deprived populations.

As Stephen Jardine wrote in 2013 ahead of the Scotland's Food and Drink conference in Perth:

> While we have world-class chefs and produce that is the envy of the world, we also have health statistics that are a national disgrace. Latest figures show 63% of Scots are overweight or obese, and that figure rises every year. Fewer than a quarter get the five-a-day fruit and vegetables considered essential for a balanced diet. [16]

To counteract the daily bombardment which most consumers are faced with we could present an alternative message, which is: eat simple fresh unprocessed seasonal fruit and vegetables. This approach could connect our health agenda with our environmental agenda and could accelerate the move away from the notion of endless consumer choice as being a social good.

Finally, there's mounting evidence that our present social and economic system is increasingly dysfunctional and inevitably is having an impact on people's access to food. Rising inequality in the UK, price increases, and the effects of the Government's austerity measures, including real time reductions in benefit payments, as well as reducing wages, mean that more people are going hungry. According to the Trussell Trust, in 2011-12 foodbanks fed 128,687 people in the UK, in 2012-13 this number will rise to over 290,000. [17] Skipping on food or going hungry is not just an issue for those on benefits. According to the *Guardian,* 'A recent report by Save the Children looked at 5,000 families with incomes of up to £30,000 a year and found that to ensure their children get enough food to eat, nearly two-thirds of parents skip meals, go into debt, avoid paying bills, and put off replacing worn-out clothing.'[18] Four out of five teachers report that about a quarter of their pupils arrive at school in the morning not having eaten enough.

In short, almost everything about food in our society is currently in crisis and it's about time that we recognised it.

'The horsemeat scandal is shocking but what's important to remember is that this isn't the system in crisis. This IS the system. In other words, this isn't the system as aberration, this is the system functioning perfectly well.'

'There's been a lot of talk about 're-establishing trust' in the food system. But that's one of the last things we need to do. . . it's a moment of opportunity for real change.'

CHAPTER TWO
Horses for courses

The absurd last-century idea that eating limitless
piles of cheap, low-grade meat and dairy was some
sort of democratic entitlement needs to be looked
upon as an aberration in world history.

Joanna Bythman

2013 opened with a shock: we were eating horsemeat and
six weeks into the scandal breaking no definitive explanation
was given to how this came about. It was in processed meat
products, in lots of them, across lots of products, lots of
brands, lots of companies. It was in schools and, well, the
truth is we really don't know how much we've eaten and where
it's been sold, never mind where it came from.

The vast procurement contracts that dominate in low-cost
low-quality British food mean that the contamination is likely
to be widespread. It's unlikely to be 'one burger' as the PR
people have repeatedly told us.

Indeed one of the largest private catering businesses in
Britain was forced to withdraw all frozen beef products across
most of its business following the discovery of horse DNA in
one of the samples it had tested.

Sodexo, which boasts of working on 2,300 sites in the UK and Ireland, declined to name the supplier of the beef product which tested positive for horse DNA. The Food Standards Agency (FSA) said the Sodexo lines affected included beef burgers, minced beef and halal minced beef.

The early arguments that horsemeat was little more than a 'trace element' or requiring 'DNA' samples now look ridiculous. The roll call of companies caught up in the scandal is impressive and testimony to how widespread the practice actually was: Tesco, Asda, Lidl, Aldi, Nestlé, Sodexo, Birds Eye, Co-op, Picard, Silvercrest Foods, Ica, Axfood, Makro, Findus, Comigel and countless others.

At the start of the fiasco these companies and their cheerleaders in the regulatory bodies made big play of it being a problem 'outwith the UK'. There have been arrests in England and Wales and we know that horsemeat was served to pupils in Scottish schools. But the reality is that this problem is rife across the continent. Products have been withdrawn in several countries: Germany, Switzerland, Belgium, Britain, France, Sweden, Ireland and the Netherlands.

The revelations have brought us a whole new terminology. After all, who had heard of 'Equidae' before this? It means the 'taxonomic family of horses and related animals'. Effectively this means horses and donkeys – 60,000 tonnes of 'Equidae' were traded by European countries in 2012.

The EU used to collect data on the slaughtering of horses but stopped in 2008 when member states made a voluntary agreement to provide this information. Since then no country has made its data available. However, in recent years, statistics have been published on the import and export of horsemeat. Though the data is incomplete, it does provide some indication of the UK's and Ireland's place in EU trade of horsemeat.[19]

The horsemeat scandal is shocking but what's important to remember is that this isn't the system in crisis. This IS the system. In other words, this isn't the system as aberration, this is the system functioning perfectly well.

What I found particularly depressing after the scandal broke was the number of foodie writers producing apparently witty articles about how horse tastes great and 'don't-we-know-people-eat-it-on-the-continent' as if this is somehow relevant. The crucial point is that they were turning a blind eye to the fact that we now have a supremely useless, largely deregulated system which means that if we are eating processed meat we don't know what we are consuming.

As food critic Joanna Blythman has pointed out the most common solution advanced during the horsemeat fiasco was to give more powers to the Food Standards Agency. But, as she points out, this would solve nothing given the FSA's track record as an industry mouthpiece:

> The first FSA boss, John Krebs, set the tone when he came into the job, endorsing the 'safety' of GM food and dismissing organic food as 'an image-led fad'. His successors have since nurtured the comfortable relationship he established with Big Food (pharmaceutical and biotech companies, global food brands, supermarket chains) while continuing to treat food campaign groups, and any organisation or voice critical of the existing food system, as the lunatic fringe.

Consequently, a top job at the FSA has marked out its incumbents not as tireless fighters for higher quality, safer food, but as prime candidates for well-paid jobs in the food industry. [20]

But there's a huge opportunity here for us in Scotland to sever the ties with this failed organisation for as the *Herald's* food writer Cate Devine points out: 'The question is, who writes the labels on our food – and who approves them?' [21]

In England, responsibility for food labelling and food safety was switched from the Food Standards Agency to the Department for Health and the Department for the Environment, Food and Rural Affairs (DEFRA) in 2010, effectively neutering the FSA's power to enforce EU food safety regulations.

In Scotland, however, the Food Standards Agency retains responsibility for food labelling and meat inspection and is accountable to the Scottish Parliament. This means the FSA has two very different roles in the UK, and this has only added to the confusion and frustration.

In fact, the Scottish Government hopes to create a new Scottish food standards body that would operate independently. A three-month consultation is taking place early in 2013 to determine its scope and responsibilities, though it probably won't come into force until 2015. [22]

Trust?

There's been a lot of talk recently about 're-establishing trust' in the food system. But that's one of the last things we need to do. We're living through a time when institutions and old systems are failing and old certainties falling by the wayside. Some call it 'collapsonomics'. It's a moment of opportunity for real change but only if we examine what's going on and resist the spin and deflection as the system attempts to inoculate itself against real change.

Writing for the *Sunday Herald* Rob Edwards revealed that as safety inspectors have lost their jobs and public spending has been slashed the sampling of food to ensure that it is safe to eat has plummeted by more than a third in Scotland over the last four years. [23]

Will Hutton writing in the *Observer* notes:

> The collapse of a belief system paralyses and terrifies in equal measure. Certainties are exploded. A reliable compass for action suddenly becomes inoperable. Everything you once thought solid vaporises. [24]

Owen Paterson, currently Secretary of State for the Environment, Food and Rural Affairs in the UK Government, appears to be living through such a nightmare and is utterly lost. As the horsemeat saga unfolded, it became more obvious by the day that the Thatcherite verities that people like Owen Paterson uphold have been shredded. The most relevant of those beliefs for our purposes are that the market is unalloyed magic, business must never be constrained by 'wealth-destroying' regulation, the state must be shrunk, and the EU is a needless collectivist project from which Britain must urgently declare independence.

But against these verities we must assert that a fundamental right in an advanced society is to know that our food is OK to eat. Quite simply we don't. Thirty years of 'slash red-tape' orthodoxy has left us eating horses when we are told we are eating beef.

The business response to the meat crisis has been predictable. The narrative has gone from 'it's a trace sample' to 'it's a rogue batch' to 'it's probably the Irish' to 'it's foreign criminals'. The Prime Minister called it a 'problem of labelling'. Now it's quite evident that it's not one burger, not one batch, not one product, not one supermarket, not one country. It's a system failure.

So re-establishing trust must be about *actually* changing our dysfunctional food system so that it's open, transparent and democratic. We do not need a PR exercise from desperate meat salesmen. But that's all we've been getting so far.

The first thing Tesco did was take out full page newspaper adverts reassuring everybody everything was ok before they knew what was going on. In its advertisement, with the headline 'We Apologise', Tesco said:

> We and our supplier have let you down and we
> apologise. People in our country will have been
> very concerned to read this morning that when they
> thought they were buying beefburgers they were
> buying something that had horse meat in it. So
> here's our promise. We will find out exactly what
> happened and, when we do, we'll come back and
> tell you.

Actually Tesco, here's our promise. How about *we* find out exactly what happened and get back to you?

Findus immediately employed Burson Marsteller, a global PR agency known for its crisis management. It has handled some of the worst PR disasters for commercial companies such as the Three Mile Island accident and Bhopal and acted for some of the world's most reviled governments and dictators. In short, it is skilled at trying to put a positive spin on disastrous events for workers or the public as well as attempting to shift blame away from those in charge.

Indeed the business response to the horsemeat scandal in the UK has been to treat it as a PR exercise. All they appear to be interested in is getting the public back to eating vast quantities of processed meats and to protect their sales and profits.

According to Tim Lang, Professor of Food Policy at City University, the Food Standards Agency which was set up in 2000 did initially improve food regulation. However, it was eviscerated by the Coalition Government in 2010 as part of the Conservatives' 'bonfire of the quangos'. Food labelling and composition are no longer part of the FSA's responsibilities and have gone back to government. The Agency's budget has also been substantially cut back. Tim Lang also argues that the FSA was once an independent voice but has become too cosy with the food industry. 'History shows that good governance requires critical internal and external voices to keep ministers informed and monitor what is happening,' he told the *Guardian,* adding: 'The coalition has restricted that capacity to audit and inspect, partly by cuts and partly by ideologically demanding a light-touch approach.' [25] It is notable that the FSA's previous chief executive, Tim Smith, is now Tesco's technical director.

Incredibly, since the horsemeat scandal broke, the FSA has been asking, Tesco-style, for companies to get back to them. It's a hopeless response from an agency that has been left with its credibility in tatters. Indeed the widespread deregulation of the food industry reflects, as Professor Tim Lang's quote suggests, the same ethic of 'light-touch' regulation which brought us the banking crisis. It is also redolent of the crisis in the media, which resulted in the Levenson Inquiry, in that there is at the heart of the horsemeat scandal a massive failure of accountability to the public.

So there's nothing to trust in a system that has allowed the wholesale corporate capture of our food culture and there's no evidence that self-regulation works. Why should it?

At the heart of this story isn't just a globalised food system where responsibility is endlessly outsourced. At its heart is a profound disrespect for all involved. Not only are live animals transported as products, but also the upper echelons of our business elite enjoy fine dining while the poorest eat horses and donkeys. So far our response has been horse jokes, business as usual or swallowing spin. The last thing we need to do is to re-establish trust.

As we saw in the last chapter, what we need are shorter supply chains, a re-evaluation of our whole relationship with the non-human world, a transparent food system that we have (some) control of and a re-localised economy that doesn't further wreck the planet. That, and a rise in expectations about what we eat.

This latest 'crisis' of a food industry that staggers from one disaster to another was inevitable. We also need to purchase our food differently. As the celebrated food writer Jay Rayner has put it: 'The horsemeat scandal is not some isolated incident. It is a symptom of a much bigger disease affecting mass food retailing in Britain.' [26]

I doubt that horsemeat causes a public health threat, though I'm sure it's a pretty clear indicator of Big Food's interest in and caring for our well-being. So the horsemeat saga can be seen as a weathervane for the lack of ethics and sustainability in the entire food supply chain.

As we disentangle this mess it's natural to wonder why Britain and Scotland have such a poor food culture and such low priorities around food? This is a complex issue, but it appears that lack of time, lack of knowledge and skills and stress all play their part. Part of this stems from our spending priorities, the rise and rise of rip-off privatised utilities and the exorbitant price of basic daily costs such as housing and transport. Natalie Bennett hits the nail on the head when she writes:

> The massive rise in the cost of housing in particular has at least in part come out of the food budget; in the two decades to 2007, the price of food for consumers fell, and the share of British household income spent on food dropped to 10%. This is clearly going to have to rise, given world food prices and the likely direction of sterling, but with our hard pressed households – already struggling with rising rents/mortgages and energy bills and leaping transport costs – it is hard to see how this is to be found. [27]

Added to this we live in a hyper-consumerist world, where identities are set around material goods and media trends.

In February 2013 it was revealed for the first time that horse had been served in school meals. Given the fast-moving processed meat 'crisis' and revelations about horse in Scottish school meals we believe the time is ripe for an urgent and fundamental re-evaluation of school meal procurement and the suspension of companies implicated in the horsemeat scandal. The response so far is utterly inadequate, defensive, undemocratic and lacking in transparency. [28]

What's required is a far more fundamental re-evaluation of school meals provision and a more robust response to this crisis.

We also need a more diverse leadership representation beyond Quality Meat Scotland on the 'expert food groups' set up by Richard Lochhead, to avoid the impression that this is the meat industry investigating the meat industry. [29]

Scotland has a historic opportunity when it launches consultation on the new FSA body in the first quarter of 2013. It's one that must have a radically different remit and outlook if we are to capitalise on the fantastic produce we have in this country. We all deserve food that's safe, healthy, good for the planet and ethically produced.

The meat problem

But we can only achieve that if we break the historic aspiration and association that 'real food' = meat. This appears to be particularly strong in cold northern countries where protein sources were historically limited and people were involved in hard physical labour. Nowadays, in a post-industrial setting this sensibility is no longer appropriate. So culturally we're attuned to eating meat but it's no longer needed.

Today, what's defined as 'the Global North' – developed countries such as the USA, Canada, Australia as well as those in Europe – are eating far too much meat and the so-called BRICS countries (Brazil, Russia, India, China and South Africa) are rapidly catching up; their aspirations fuelled by the status associated with eating meat in Western culture.

The consequences of large scale meat production and consumption have been well documented, most recently in a United Nations Environment Programme (UNEP) commissioned report *Our Nutrient World: The challenge to produce more food and energy with less pollution* (2013), which calls on the Global North to halve its meat consumption. The message is slowly starting to resonate with policy makers. The Swedish Government, for example, has just proposed a tax on meat in an attempt to lower its consumption.

This shift would require innovation in what we grow in Scotland and how we source and prepare food. If countries continue to subsidise and support meat and dairy producers but not those involved in the production of fruit and vegetables then it's hardly surprising that we end up with a food market saturated with meat and dairy. Indeed we currently have a commercial cartel with a vested interest in promoting processed meat and ready meals and a subsidised farming industry heavily focused on beef, pork, mutton and lamb.

This argument does not derive from squeamishness about meat eating. It is not premised on being 'anti-business'. It is simply about trying to reverse the over-use of meat in Western diets. This change will also be beneficial to health as eating large quantities of meat, particularly processed meat, is harmful to health and is linked to heart disease and various cancers.

Even in rich countries most people ate significantly less meat one or two generations ago. This is why meat used to be savoured and respected. Expensive meat like a roast chicken or a joint was often kept for Sundays or special occasions. In the past decades our quest for ever cheaper meat, which we can then consume more often and in large quantities, has resulted in a massive expansion of intensively farmed livestock. This has diverted vast quantities of grain from human to animal consumption, and concomitantly has required intensive use of fertilisers, pesticides and herbicides. According to the UNEP report, this has 'caused a web of water and air pollution that is damaging human health'. [30]

The further knock-on effect is a run-off from these chemicals which is creating dead zones in the seas, causing toxic algal blooms and killing fish. Some chemicals are threatening bees, amphibians and destabilising sensitive ecosystems.

In the words of Mark Sutton, author of *Our Nutrient World* 'Society must think about livestock and food choices much more, for the environment and health.' [31]

His answer is more vegetables on our plate, and less animal protein. 'Eat meat, but less often – make it special,' he urged. 'Portion size is key. Many portions are too big, more than you want to eat. Think about a change of culture that says, "I like the taste, but I don't need so much of it".' [32]

'The dominance of big supermarkets encourages not just centralisation but giantism in the whole food system. . . large plant bakeries supply over 90% of the UK market whereas in Italy craft bakers supply over 90% of bread.'

CHAPTER THREE

Big Shopping

The fact is that British supermarkets are reliant on similar systems for many of their products. The supermarkets have assumed that they didn't need to think about the producers of their goods, could always buy cheaply on the world market, ship in cheaply (without considering the real environmental costs of those food miles) – to treat food like a commodity like oil or iron ore.

Natalie Bennett

If we really want to change our relationship with food and the whole food system we need to change not just regulation of the supply chain, we also need to regain control of retail. There are just over 8,000 supermarkets in the UK and they account for 97% of total grocery sales. Tesco, Sainsbury's, Asda and Morrisons together take 76% of that market. Their share of non-food retailing currently stands at 14%, a figure up by a staggering 75% since 2003.

In Britain a new Tesco, Morrisons, Sainsbury's or Asda opens every other day. Tesco alone now controls over 30% of the grocery market in the UK. One pound in every seven spent in Britain goes to Tesco alone. In 2012, the supermarket chain announced profits of £3.8bn. It is intersting to note that profits fell to just under £2bn in 2013.

Nonetheless that's a staggering monopoly and it has been allowed to happen as the result of a lack of political will and imagination, a totally flawed concept of 'jobs' and growth in the economy and the subtle but all pervasive influence big business can have over political parties' policies as a result of relentless lobbying and ready access to Ministers.

The supermarkets are clear about what they want from Government. As Tesco's Sir Terry Leahy put it: 'What saps our strength are high taxes: excessive regulations; inflexible working practices; and the gold plating of EU directives. All of this undermines British businesses on the home front as they battle in global markets.' [33]

What does this monopoly look like on the ground, in one region?

In Fife the annual supermarket turnover in 2009 was £500.5 million (approximately 79.5% of retail spending on food in Fife) while the local food market via farmers markets and farm shops account for only 0.52% of the total sales, and estimates for the UK are similar. Fair competition and alternative market routes are needed to develop the local food system.

Nonetheless, the local food movement in Scotland is flourishing with community food initiatives of all sorts expanding throughout rural and urban areas – many of them funded by the Scottish Government's Climate Challenge Fund (CCF). According to a recent survey the number of Scottish people trying to buy local food is increasing and 54% and 49% of the respondents said that their main reason for buying local food was to support local producers and local retailers respectively. What's more, 40% stated that buying local food helps to keep jobs in the area. [34]

The technical name for this is 'the local multiplier effect': it is a measure of how money is respent locally instead of shifting profits to shareholders, insurance companies or management. The New Economics Foundation compared the multiplier effects of buying fruits and vegetables from an organic box scheme versus getting the same items for supermarket in an area of Cornwall. The results showed that every £10 spent on the veg box generated £25 for the local economy as opposed to £14 generated by buying in the supermarket.[35]

Growing evidence indicates that the success of the major supermarkets is partly based on trading practices that have serious, negative effects on suppliers, farmers and workers worldwide, local shops and the environment. [36] They have continued to assume that they would always be able to buy what they needed at a price that suited them, from all points of the globe. As a result, they did not care that the bad deals they were giving to British farmers were forcing them out of business and destroying the country's agricultural self-sufficiency.

Last year's row over falling payments to dairy farmers shows the extent of the problem. The *Scottish Farmer* reported that Lord Morris of Aberavon said he had 'serious concerns' for the actual survival of the UK dairy sector. He made these remarks at the opening of the new Farmer's Union of Wales's pavilion on the Royal Welsh showground in summer 2012. Lord Morris, who was their first deputy general secretary and legal adviser, said:

> The major supermarkets hold the industry in their grip but some have been less fair than others to their discredit. In their own interests do they really want the dairy industry to die? . . . There is something completely wrong when a pint of milk is about 50p and a pint of water 83p . . . The Westminster minister of agriculture is trying to agree a voluntary code of practice with the dairy and retail industries and to work with them to ensure stability in the market. . . . But in a deregulatory age this is the only offer on the table and I wish the minister well, though time is not on his side for it to succeed. The whole supply chain needs repair. [37]

Dairy industry commentator Ian Potter welcomed the peer's comments, agreeing that the current supply chain was both 'wrong and immoral'. 'There's the obvious to start with – the obscenely unfair share of the margins,' he told the *Scottish Farmer*, adding:

> But there are other unseen shady activities too. How many 'back door' payments do retailers force processors to make, for example? The ones I am told about make my eyes water, let alone theirs. . . The bottom line is dairy farmers and processors are paying for cheap milk, for this immoral activity and wanton greed. [38]

As an example of how milk sales were being manipulated by retailers Mr Potter pointed out that Tesco were that week offering two free pints of milk to every customer purchasing 1kg of a particular brand of margarine.

Successive governments have hardly interfered with how the supermarkets go about their business. The long-fought-for groceries ombudsman, promised in the 2010 election manifestos, will not be in place until 2014 at the earliest and who knows how much power he or she will wield.

As we in the Fife Diet project wrote in the New Food Manifesto (Fife Diet, 2012):

> The Competition Commission has discussed the effect of supermarkets on local jobs, and research has shown that every time a new supermarket opens an average of 276 local jobs are lost in the mid/long term. Recently, we have seen how the controversial Workfare programme of the UK Coalition Government has re-opened the debate around low paid, part time jobs and the poor quality of jobs offered by the big retailers. [39]

Competition policy is currently a matter reserved to Westminster. In UK legislation a monopoly is any one business group that controls more than 30% of a product market, exactly in line with the market share of Tesco, who are the largest retailer in the UK.

It's unlikely this will change under Westminster and it's another compelling reason for Scottish independence.

The extent of what's termed 'corporate capture' of our food system is something to which most of us are completely blind. It's happened by stealth over the last thirty years and is now something we don't consider at all. Even questioning it can make people appear as if they are cranks or uncomfortably out on a limb.

For example, why do we accept that McDonald's still sponsor youth football in Scotland when we have a major problem with childhood obesity and ill health? And given that some of its products were found to contain horsemeat why is Asda one of the sponsors for Scotland's Food and Drink Excellence Awards?

The dominance of big supermarkets encourages not just centralisation but giantism in the whole food system. In the UK six processors (Arla/Express, Dairy Crest, Robert Wiseman, Glanbia, Associated Co-operative Creameries and Nestlé) control 93% of UK dairy processing and six supermarkets control 65% of liquid milk sales. All these companies use centralised systems of production and distribution. Corporations such as Danone either build large 1,000 cows farms or encourage co-operatives to increase their numbers and the size of the farms that supply them.[40] In Scotland, the number of small dairyfarms is falling every year: from 2,000 in 1999 to 1,300 now. Small dairies only survive if they can organise their own bottling and supply customers directly, or if they can add value on the farm through cheese or ice cream production.

Just two companies, Rank Hovis (part of Tomkins PLC) and Archer Daniels Midland Milling, account for more than 50% of bread flour milled in the UK – the third largest cereal producer in the EU after France and Germany. In 2005 12% of the UK's cereal area was in Scotland. The main cereal crop in Scotland is barley of which 34% goes into malting and 54% for animal feed. Milled wheat grown in Scotland is mainly used for biscuit making, distilling and animal feed. It is, therefore, unlikely that very much of the cereal grown is milled locally for food consumption. The technology for milling cereals on a farm scale is available but centralised plants are the norm. Large plant bakeries supply over 90% of the UK market whereas in Italy craft bakers supply over 90% of bread.

Food waste

At the beginning of 2013 the whole media suddenly woke up to one of the most obscene aspects of the current food system – the issue of food waste. How did that happen? It resulted from the publication of a report by the Institution of Mechanical Engineers (IME) which blamed poor storage, strict sell-by dates and fussy consumers for the huge piles of food discarded each year in the Western world. [41]

In the media frenzy that followed no-one appeared to be fingering the role of supermarkets. One notable exception was the *Herald's* film writer, Alison Rowat, who wrote:

> Due to supermarkets imposing strict standards on size, shape and colour, anything out of the ordinary is rejected. The IME reckons 30% of the UK's vegetable crop is turned down for such reasons. How do we like them apples? Not much is the answer. It is a scandal which exposes Western attitudes to food, the dominance of supermarkets and our general reluctance to value the simple and wholesome over the expensive and manufactured. [42]

Most other commentators focused on us dumb consumers. But the reality is that we have allowed a few companies, 'the big four', to utterly dominate our food system. Now we stand dazed and confused at the obscenity of food waste. We shouldn't be: that's the system. Supermarkets are designed to get you to buy stuff you don't need. That's how they make their money. Why is this a surprise?

So let's get angry about food waste. But we need to keep asking: who controls the food system? And, as we have just seen, it is supermarkets as they are now responsible for 97% of total grocery sales in the UK.

It is interesting to ask if there is a hierarchy to what we could call 'structured profligacy'? According to Tristram Stuart, author of *Waste: Uncovering the Global Food Scandal* (2009) there is. He writes:

> The Co-op is the best performing supermarket, 27% more efficient than average. Sainsbury's is the worst, apparently 14% more wasteful than the average and 55% worse than the Co-op. Morrisons and Tesco are about average and Waitrose and Asda are slightly more wasteful than average and around 47% worse than the Co-op. [43]

Is there a better way? Of course there is. In Japan and Taiwan the government requires food businesses to reduce food waste by 65%. They also feed waste to their pigs, a practice we banned after the Foot and Mouth outbreak: a classic example of our dysfunctional food system turning in on itself. We can't do something that is common sense because the rest of our food system is so rotten.

In the UK we throw away 8.3 million tonnes of food from our homes every year. Wasting food costs the average family with children £680 a year, or £50 a month. If we all stop wasting food that could have been eaten, the CO_2 impact would be the equivalent of taking one in four cars off the road.

Here are three 'killer' food waste facts:

• There are nearly one billion malnourished people in the world, and approximately 40 million tonnes of food wasted by US households, retailers and food services each year would be enough to satisfy the hunger of every one of them.

• If we planted trees on land currently used to grow unnecessary surplus and wasted food, this would offset a theoretical maximum of 100% of greenhouse gas emissions from fossil fuel combustion.

• All the world's nearly one billion hungry people could be lifted out of malnourishment on less than a quarter of the food that is wasted in the US, UK and Europe.

It's important to recognise that this type of waste is built into the system: waste is neither the result of our own inherent stupidity or selfishness, it's the whole point of the system. For example, if you bought chickens on a two for one deal and threw one of then out, who cares? The important thing is that you *bought* them, not that you ate them. Indeed the whole ethos of supermarkets is to get people to buy more and more stuff even though they don't need it.

It is also worth remembering that Methane, gas from the waste produced by animals, is 25 times more potent a greenhouse gas than CO_2. So, food waste is not just about ethics or hunger it's also about climate change.

Consumer choice

One of the fundamental beliefs in Western culture is that 'choice' is synonymous with freedom. Our ability as consumers to choose from a myriad of goods, services, or ways to spend our time is seen as symbolic of our freedom and autonomy. As supermarkets have massively increased people's consumer choices it's commonplace to believe that this is beneficial.

But is choice such a positive thing in our lives? An American psychologist called Professor Barry Schwartz has made a particular study of choice and its impact on our well-being. He sets out his findings in *The Paradox of Choice: Why More is Less* (2004).

In a bid to quantify the bewildering range of choices we face every day, Schwartz went to his local supermarket (not a particularly large one by American standards, he tells us) and started calculating his choices. He found that he could choose from:

85 varieties and brands of cracker, some with sodium, some without; some fat-free, others with fat; normal size and bite-size

285 different sorts of biscuits (or cookies)

13 'sports' drinks

65 'box drinks' aimed at children

85 other flavours,

75 iced teas and adult drinks

95 types of snacks like crisps, tacos or Pringles

61 varieties of sun oil and sun block

150 lipsticks

360 types of shampoo, gel and mousse

275 types of cereal

230 soups, including 29 different chicken soups.

Everywhere he looked his choices continued to expand – from 55 different salad options to a range of different dental flosses. It was the same, if not worse, when he looked at electrical gadgets. He calculated that the confusing array of stereo tuners, CD players, tape players and speakers added up to the opportunity to create more than 6.5 million different stereo systems by mixing and matching the various elements.

Schwartz recounts experiments which show that when people are given numerous choices they feel stressed and often don't choose anything. For example, in one experiment people were given the opportunity to sample upmarket jams and then buy one at a good discount. But people simply did not avail themselves of the opportunity once they had a choice of six or more flavours. Why? Because making a choice was stressful and so the tasters just gave up, and moved on.

Schwartz argues that instead of liberating us, having to select from myriad choices can paralyse us, rendering us incapable of deciding which holiday, pension plan, electricity supplier, type of jeans, or jam will meet our needs or wants. Indeed he argues that 'choice overload' makes us question our decisions before we even make them.

And even when we do make a choice, we tend to be less satisfied, fearing that there was an even better stereo, car or ready meal out there which we failed to choose. In the 1950s and 1960s when choice was limited, we could blame manufacturers, retailers or even the government if we bought a TV, chunk of cheese, or pension which didn't turn out to be what we wanted. But faced with infinite choices we blame ourselves when the purchase doesn't fully satisfy us. It also sets us up for unrealistically high expectations.

In the long run, excessive choice can lead to decision-making paralysis, anxiety and perpetual stress. Self-blame can also lead to a reduction in our sense of well-being and happiness. Indeed Schwartz argues that in a culture that tells us there's no excuse for falling short of perfection when your options are limitless, too much choice can lead to clinical depression.

The core message from Barry Schwartz's work is that some amount of choice in our lives is good as it affords us some personal autonomy and expression. However, we're mistaken if we think that because some choice is good, more is even better. It's not as it's often debilitating.

Barry Schwartz argues that to improve happiness in Western countries we should try to restrict our choices and also lower our expectations: paradoxically it's when we're not aiming for the best, and don't have high expectations, that we can be pleasantly surprised and able to feel satisfied and happy.

The New Economics Foundation and local economy

There's a real irony that while supermarkets offer 'endless choice' within their stores they do so from a supreme monopoly of retailing. But the reality of a retail landscape dominated by just four companies is disastrous for local economies.

As the research from the New Economics Foundation has proved, supermarkets suck the life out of towns, hoovering up money and extracting it from the local economy. The result is there for us all to see:

We used to be a nation of shop-keepers. We have

become a nation of shop-busters. Local shops and services – including corners shops, grocers, high-street banks, post offices, pubs, hardware stores – are fast disappearing. The change is happening most visibly in villages and market towns, but just as dramatically in many larger urban and suburban areas. Between 1995-2000, we lost roughly one-fifth of these vital institutions – the very fabric of our local economies. If current trends continue, we will lose a third of the tattered remains of that fabric over the next ten years. The result is Ghost Town Britain – an increasing number of communities and neighbourhoods that lack easy access to local banks, post offices, corner shops and pubs that provide the social glue that holds communities together. [44]

So what's the alternative? The alternative is to allow a diverse range of business, social enterprises, co-ops and new structures to flourish away from the grip of Big Retail. This inevitably leads to a more creative small-scaled growth of innovation and services creating a richer retail experience, and often, better food.

To do this we need take on the power of the supermarkets, first by halting their expanding monopoly and then beginning to slowly roll back their domination of our economy.

'The reality is that people are going hungry today not because there is not enough food [in the world], but because they are poor and cannot afford food.'

'Glut and excess are also at the heart of our food system. For example, with just nine workers, one chicken factory can produce 10 million kilos of chicken meat a year in 'sheds' containing 54,000 birds.'

CHAPTER FOUR
Living within limits

> What difference does it make how much is laid
> away in a man's safe or in his barns, how many
> head of stock he grazes or how much capital he
> puts out at interest, if he is always after what is
> another's and only counts what he has yet to get,
> never what he has already? You ask what is the
> proper limit to a person's wealth? First, having what
> is essential, and second, having what is enough.
>
> Lucius Seneca, 4BC–AD65

As discussed in the last chapter, the idea of restricting your choice is an anathema to modern society which has the following equation at its core: choice is good, more choice is better, endless choice is best. This in all things. Limits are bad, wrong and belong to the past. No wonder we have lost the concept of 'enough'.

The idea of living within limits, defined by where you live, is something that the vast majority of the world lives with, and in this country we lived with until thirty or forty years ago. But it has rapidly become something extraordinary.

The present food crisis, in which nearly a billion people are going hungry is used as proof of 'food scarcity' plaguing the planet. This idea is reflected in the endless mantra on public forums that 'the world must increase food production or there will be mass starvation'. The reality is that people are going hungry today not because there is not enough food, but because they are poor and cannot afford food to eat.

The world produces one and a half times enough food to feed every man, woman and child currently living. Studies show that sustainable agricultural practices can produce enough food to feed 10 billion people, the planet's expected peak population.[45] However, given how quickly climate change is affecting agriculture worldwide, these assumptions may be revised. [46]

Living within place and continuing to inhabit cities is an essential part of re-negotiating our relationship to the natural world. What is essential is a process of shifting from a globalised food economy to a bioregional food culture.

A bioregion is a land and water territory whose limits are defined not by political boundaries, but by the geographical limits of human communities and ecological systems. For the purposes of Scotland you can imagine a series of regions like Tayside, Fife, Argyll, Strathclyde, the Clyde valley and so on. That such an approach is almost impossible for people to conceive of, never mind actively support, doesn't mean that it's not the right approach to take.

The Fife Diet

We've been eating locally in Fife in an active co-ordinated way since 2007. When we started the media interest was instant and constant. At our launch a live television camera crew came to film us. On reflection this was bizarre. That 'eating food that is grown near where you live' can become a news story is an incredible thing in itself. It's not only what humans have all done for more than ten thousand years, it is what the vast majority of people around the world do to this day. Where's the story?

In the mad world we live in however the idea of eating food from near where you live is ground-breaking and extraordinary. Dozens of us chose to eat this way for a year, from October 2007 and have decided to continue to do so. We are choosing this option mostly out of a real sense that climate change and peak oil, and various multiple dysfunction-alities of our food system, are converging to mean that eating locally is the way of the future. From the initial 14 or so that decided to try this, the group has grown and grown and now numbers over 5000.

The idea was never to try and eat 100% regionally. That would be very hard and I'm not sure what it would achieve. Our goal was to eat 80% from the local area and 20% from further afield. The idea was to really know your food region (what the French call the *terroir*), to celebrate what you *could* grow, rear and land here, and explore what your place could produce.

So, what did we eat and what did we miss?

We ate seasonally and we ate what could be easily produced here – without excessive artificial heating and, for the most part, without pesticides.

At the end of the first year we polled participants and here are some of their responses.

Sam from Rosyth ate: 'potatoes, carrots, onions, pork, beef, venison, beans, lettuce, spinach, tomatoes, pumpkin, ice cream, butter, oats'.

Wendy from Dunshelt wrote: 'We found meat the easiest with Fletcher's venison, Jamesfield beef and pork from a small holding near Kinghorn, also pheasant and rabbit when available. Vegetables from Bellfield supplemented by produce from Pillars and what we grew ourselves. Fruit locally when in season and often foraged. Eggs from our own chickens.'

Adam ate a vegan diet and grew a lot of his own food. Others ate 'what my granny cooked': mince and tatties, soups, scones, soda bread, bangers and mash, stews, pies, casseroles – traditional stuff.

Andrew from Rosyth wrote: 'This town used to be a Garden City (1915-1918) and we began to re-examine the town's heritage and re-think its future. At the moment it has lots of unemployment and dependency on the military.'

Angus from Lochgelly wrote of: 'Understanding for the first time what it would mean to live here, to actually live here in this place in this time. I felt re-rooted.'

Another participant from Inverkeithing wrote of eating 'Meat – beef, buffalo, chicken, lamb, pork, venison from the farmers' market. Fish – various fresh from Inverkeithing, and kippers from St Monans. Veg from the veg box. Fruit from the farmers' market. Also eggs, honey, cheese.'

So it's a diet that is made up almost entirely of unprocessed foods. We ate probably double the '5 a day' of fruit and veg (though admittedly fruit of a more limited range than the 365 days a year supermarket shopper). We ate a low (but high quality) meat diet, sourced from farms we knew well and trusted. It is important to point out that this type of diet contains a number of superfoods: mackerel, oats, kale and raspberries to name a few.

What did we miss? The ease of ripping open a packaged pizza and ten minutes later chewing on some rubbery hydrogenated tomato product was something we yearned for at first. But the 'convenience' of this type of food is predicated on a lifestyle where you are lashed to the job and confined to a treadmill. Fast foods can be replaced. Instead of pizza we had omelettes and frittata. We kept coffee, tea and sugar and debated the best type of vegetable oils. Much of the rape seed oils we tried seemed poor quality and pesticide dependent.

It was easy enough to source the vast bulk of our food from the region of Fife. Beer from Clackmannanshire and wine from Perthshire constituted welcome 'contraband' goods.

Fife is blessed with good food, but not super-blessed. Lots of people I've spoken to have said something like, 'Of course you can do this in Fife but you couldn't do this where I live'. But this is a bit of a cop-out. Argyll, the Highlands and the North-East have fishing catches that would make Fifers jealous. Many cities have better bakeries than we could ever dream of and surrounding regions that could easily provide wheat. Ayrshire boasts better dairy produce than Fife and Perthshire and Tayside have some of the best soft fruit in Europe.

We've conned ourselves into believing that we're the Poor Man of Europe when in fact we have a fantastic range of food here in Scotland. We've told (and heard) too many gags about 'deep fried Mars bars', and it's time we woke up to some of the fantastic food we produce in Scotland. That's why some of the best of it gets exported (seafood particularly) directly to France, Spain, Portugal and Italy.

To make a start we need to know more about our regions again and what they can produce. We need to re-learn how to grow and cook together, how to pickle, preserve and bottle, as well as how we can exchange the things we long for, but can't grow here – for some of our own delicacies. This might all be a struggle but the truth is we can't achieve a low or zero carbon society by transporting food about the world as if nature, the changing seasons, or 'place' don't exist at all.

It's difficult to get 'balance' in a world that is so out of kilter. We found that as we entered the 'hungry gap' – that time between spring foods becoming available and the drop-off of winter veg – eating locally can seem hard. It is. It is especially hard when you are doing it in a society that doesn't even recognise the importance of what you are doing. However, it was also good to know that we were not alone.

Growing communities

The Fife Diet emerged around the same time and with a lot of the same thinking as Growing Communities in London. In fact we seemed to hit on the 80/20 idea together. Growing Communities have managed to produce an amazing graphic that describes it.

Some people come to eating locally rationally, some people instinctively. It doesn't matter. This isn't about purity, it's about clarity. Eat local and seasonal. When you can't then show solidarity through fair and feral trade.

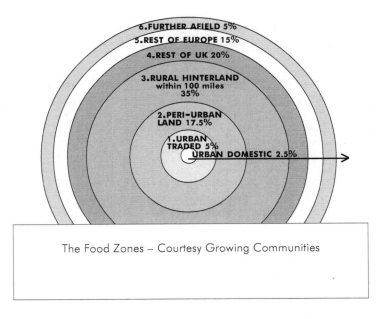

The Food Zones – Courtesy Growing Communities

The important thing is not to focus on the 80/20 equation but the criteria. Why would you choose something from further afield? There are good and bad reasons. Growing Communities explains:

> The Food Zones shows what type of food could best come from where and is an initial attempt to illustrate what percentage of our food we might aim to source from different zones: starting with the urban areas in which most of us live and applying a kind of food subsidiarity – raising what it is best to raise as close as we can and then moving outwards taking into account the **principles** outlined earlier and the **factors** shown below.
>
> Growing Communities has a wider vision of what a sustainable, resilient food system might look like

which encompasses our key principles while aiming to reduce the amount of oil and fossil fuels it takes to feed us.

Our vision can be expressed in the form of a diagram – the Growing Communities' Food Zones. It shows what type of food could best come from where and is an initial attempt to illustrate what percentage of our food we need to source from different zones.

It starts with the urban areas in which most of us live and moves outwards applying a kind of food subsidiarity. Raising what we can as close as we can taking into account a number of factors, e.g. soil type, climate, what grows best where, size of plots available, infrastructure and transport links available, the degree of mechanisation that makes most sense, and the perishability of the produce.

It's based on human-scale, organic, mixed farms located in and around urban areas which are directly connected to the urban communities they feed and which enable those communities to source increasing amounts of food from close to where they live.

It's built around the idea of community sized 'building blocks' which encompass positive but appropriately scaled trading relationships starting from the local and working out to global and which enable urban producers, small farmers, producer co-ops, larger farms and food imports to exist in harmony.

Enough versus excess

The idea behind this kind of local eating is not so much self-sufficiency, as 'sufficiency'. Living within limits. As we saw in the last chapter this may seem difficult and dull but it is in fact liberating.

However, there's little doubt that it flies in the face of the current ethos of our day. People are not encouraged to accept constraints of any kind and certainly not those imposed by nature. The rise in cosmetic surgery is testimony to this. Through their exposure to the mass media women are continually urged to defy the process of ageing with Botox injections or plastic surgery.

What's more, consumption is not about having enough for a comfortable, secure life. Conspicuous consumption and excess are increasingly at the very heart of the system. The distinguished economist, Robert Frank, describes this phenomenon as 'luxury fever' and the British psychotherapist Oliver James calls it 'affluenza'. [47] Even ordinary people on middling incomes now aspire to the lifestyle once reserved for the rich and famous – luxury cruises, Christmas shopping trips to New York, designer clothes . . . the list is endless. The tragedy is that, as prices rise and wage levels remain stagnant, ordinary people may aspire to a luxurious lifestyle yet their real standard of living is falling. Meanwhile the rich take more and more of national income. Indeed inequality in the UK is back at levels that pertained in the mid nineteenth century. This is why we can pick up a newspaper and read of the growth of food banks in twenty first century Britain as well as a review of a Bentley Continental costing £176,385 with a sound system which alone is worth £5,365.

Glut and excess are also at the heart of our food system. For example, with just nine workers, one chicken factory can produce 10 million kilos of chicken meat a year in 'sheds' containing 54,000 birds.

So nowadays there are very few models of acceptance, working with nature or choosing appropriate models and systems. But we need to create them.

How do we move to a bioregional approach? The answer Kirkpatrick Sale gives is 'remembrance and invention'. Or, as Growing Communities in Hackney puts it, 'remember a food tradition, and invent a new one.'

'Scotland's local food revolution is packed with examples of innovative community projects up and down the land.'

CHAPTER FIVE

Community through food

> The corporatisation of something as intimate as eating is, for many of us today, a good place to draw the line.
>
> Michael Pollan

One of the signs at Ikea reads: 'Too tired to cook?' On the menu are meat balls which we know, for a while anyway, contained horsemeat. This Ikea experience is the apogee of beautifully designed but ultimately low-quality contemporary living. Everything looks good but isn't. Somehow it sums up a society that has run out of time, and money and has lost a sense of value.

We've certainly lost the sense that eating food is a social activity. The idea of sharing food as the most basic act of conviviality has been lost by many of us in modern society as we're now too stressed, or too isolated, to open our homes or share our tables. People regularly sit at home, often on their own, eating bland ready meals whilst watching food or dining programmes on television.

The most important lesson we've learnt from the Fife Diet experiment is that people are yearning for a sense of togetherness and nothing satisfies this need more than eating food together. If that food can be prepared together too, so that no-one is 'playing host' then the experience is richer still. On one level this sounds trite and superficial yet the experience in rural Fife was profound. What's going on?

What people experienced at the 'community lunches' we organisd in the early days of the Fife Diet experiment was a simple act of sharing, a mutualism that's a rare gift in a society dominated by commodities and materialism. No-one was trying to sell anyone anything. Another important factor is that people stepped out of their domestic sphere into a public realm and interacted with their peers as adults and equals. This wasn't a mediated experience. This wasn't online. They also discussed and exchanged views about subjects that are heartfelt.

Often our media and our celebrity culture reduces us to an infantile state. In our modern world we rarely seem to meet and discuss issues of some substance on an equal footing. This doesn't mean it has to be a dry and super-serious experience. One of the most successful recent community development projects I've come across was **Letham Nights**, a travelling inn in northern Fife that acted as a pop-up pub, with musicians, locally brewed ale and good food.

Scotland's local food revolution is packed with examples of similarly innovative community projects up and down the land. Here's a flavour of a few of them.

Community food projects

In 2012 in the south side of Glasgow, Reuben Chesters opened **Locavore**, a food co-op to promote food growing, cookery and sustainable local food. He stated simply:

> We believe we need to rethink our relationship with food, from the way it is produced to the way it is cooked, eaten, and disposed of. By changing our relationship with food we can reduce the negative impact food has on the environment while improving our health, our economy, our community and our happiness! [48]

Locavore projects already include 'edible platforms' at railway stations on the south side of Glasgow , running regular gardening and food events such as workshops and hosting volunteer opportunities.

The outlet also doubles as a community kitchen where regular sessions and workshops are held on getting the very best out of local seasonal ingredients, lessons in making jam and preserves, how to cook with wild food, and how to make your own wine. While it's a tiny operation it's projects like Locavore that are at the heart of the new food economy. They're about young people completely rejecting the values they've been handed down and starting with a clean slate.

In Edinburgh the **Grassmarket Community Project** has taken the idea of the Soup Kitchen and turned it on its head. The project is a partnership between the Grassmarket Mission and Greyfriars Kirk. It focuses on adults who are facing 'deep social exclusion' and have been marginalised by lack of opportunity, skills and aspiration.

Two of their projects use food as the tool for change. Jocelyn Lockhart runs the Herb Garden. Among the gravestones in Greyfriars Kirkyard, volunteers have planted over 200 medicinal and culinary herbs. Prior to the establishment of the kirkyard after the Scottish Reformation, a Franciscan Friary and apothecary garden occupied the site. Trying to establish links with history, the group works together to maintain over six beds, including two traditional medicinal beds, two culinary beds, and a dyers' bed.

Plough to Plate combines cookery classes and gardening in an exciting new local food project. This initiative sees participants taking part in gardening activity at the Royal Edinburgh Community Gardens as well as basic cookery training within the Grassmarket Centre's own teaching kitchen. The aim is to link individuals normally detached from the food system to the entire process, from 'plough to plate'. An important element in this programme is the communal meal at the end of each cooking session where the cooks have the opportunity to share their work with participants in some of the other projects.

Sometimes the food movement in Scotland has been guilty of operating in silos: environmental, organic, local, slow, healthy, without realising common cause. But the Grassmarket group don't see themselves as detached from the wider movement. The Grassmarket Community Project hopes to facilitate a more resilient food system in Scotland and aspires to work as closely as possible with organic growers and farmers in the local area. Many of these farmers are very supportive of the project and believe strongly in what they are doing. These relationships have helped them achieve a food programme that is 60% organic and 80% local.

In the west of Scotland, groups like the **East Kilbride Development Trust** have pioneered good practice by encouraging and re-skilling people to grow some of their own food, save seeds and reclaim land. Since 2008, with an incredible amount of input from local, volunteer manpower, the trust has created the Scottish Seed Exchange Network and they distributed a staggering 20,000 packets of open pollinated vegetable seeds free in the first year. They have also taught courses in growing food, composting, bee keeping and chicken rearing. They've put raised beds, wormeries and advanced composting in thirty schools across the area. That's a phenomenal effort and one that defies the lazy stereotype that this type of activity is a middle class obsession.

Another ground-breaking community project is **SAGE [Sow and Grow Everywhere]**, a visionary initiative to generate a massive change in community food growing in Glasgow and the Clyde Valley. It is run by the arts organisation NVA. The project's conceptual breakthrough was the use of portable temporary gardens, often in contaminated or vacant urban plots. This approach by-passed the sort of planning regulations that have plagued allotment schemes for decades. As they say themselves:

> SAGE is allowing people with no previous experience of growing their own food and herbs to both provide for their families, friends and potentially offer surplus to a wider area. It is complementing, supporting and extending the existing network of community food initiatives. SAGE also offers the potential for the larger initiatives to be developed into vibrant social enterprises. [49]

SAGE projects were developed at Bellsmyre Community

Garden; West Dunbartonshire; Shettleston Community Growing Project; the Concrete Garden, Possil; Blyth-Spirit Community; Greyfriars Garden; Shuttle Street, Glasgow; Partick GAP Growing Project; GHLN Community Garden; SAGE Sighthill; and SAGE Cranhill.

In 2003 Greig Robertson (an Edinburgh based social entrepreneur) conceived and developed the **Edinburgh Community Backgreens Initiative** (ECBI) following a research trip to Denmark and Sweden. In 2004, Greig promoted the community backgreen model to housing associations around Scotland. This resulted in the development of a feasibility study with Canmore Housing Association into the relevance of the model to the Scottish context.

The target area for the study was the Gorgie and Dalry area of Edinburgh as this was Canmore Housing Association's traditional area of operation. The study found that 20% of backgreens were practically derelict and a further 50% were not meeting their potential. The study also resulted in the identification of pilot sites and the further development of the community backgreens model.

Funds were raised to start work at two pilot sites, in Wheatfield and Cherrytree. Residents around each site were invited to participate in volunteer workshops to regenerate the backgreens – approximately 45 households participated at both sites. Design workshops were held at each site during November and December 2005.

Participants reached agreement on the types of features that would be put in place at each site. This together with the research carried out during the feasibility study and the earlier research in Denmark, formed the basis of the community backgreens model.

In 2007 ECBI started working at five new community sites in Gorgie Dalry, Caleys, Orwell, Appletree, Murieston, and Slateford whilst work continued at the two pilot sites, Cherrytree and Wheatfield. Now the project has developed a new strand with a huge amount of work to be undertaken in a project called 'Edible Estates' working in Wester Hailes.

FareShare Goes Local! is a Community Food Initiative North East (CFINE) project, based in Aberdeen. It builds on contacts with local north east stores and growers to negotiate collection and distribution of their surplus produce which would normally go to landfill. The project distributes the produce to low income, vulnerable, homeless and disabled community members. The community's carbon footprint is set to decrease as the surplus local food supplies, previously destined for waste, are distributed for local consumption. The project also creates opportunities for volunteering and work placements as well as raising awareness of food's carbon footprint and the facts about climate change.

The significance of this project cannot be underestimated and not just because of its scale: this is the first time that any social project, previously focusing on food poverty, has taken up a climate change agenda.

All the projects listed above – involve thousands of people. But there are countless thousands more who grow their own food without being part of any formal project. And what's most interesting is that the numbers have risen substantially in recent years. DEFRA's *Food 2030* report (2009) produced data which shows that about one in three people grow some of their own food in Scotland. This varies wildly from 'some tomatoes' or some window-sill herbs to a full sized allotment, but the intent remains the same. Evidence is unreliable but the growth of garden centres and seed sales is one indication there is currently a huge boom in 'grow your own'. Another indication is the fact that there are over 100,000 people waiting for access to allotments in the UK. This trend is borne out in other countries as well such as the success of Ireland's grow-it-yourself movement led by Mick Kelly.

As more people become interested in using land or growing food and this movement really begins to build, other things will happen. With experience people are going to get better at growing, better at creating community food networks, and better at sharing and swapping seeds and knowledge. It is a far cry from the ethos of the traditional garden centre or BBC gardening programmes with their emphasis on ornamental plants and dependence on chemicals.

These very different attempts to wrestle control over land and enhance aspects of our food-growing capacity should be seen as part of an international movement, that's known elsewhere as 'food sovereignty'. And this movement is likely to become a major agent of change.

Indeed while food relocalisation is decried by some as a retreat into parochialism, it is in fact an act of international solidarity, and one that sees common cause with groups and peasant movements across the globe.

> Food sovereignty is the right of peoples to healthy and culturally appropriate food produced through ecologically sound and sustainable methods, and

their right to define their own food and agriculture systems. It puts those who produce, distribute and consume food at the heart of food systems and policies rather than the demands of markets and corporations. It defends the interests and inclusion of the next generation. [50]

So reads the Declaration of Nyéléni, following discussion in 2007 on the importance of food sovereignty at a forum comprising 500 representatives from peasant and family farmers, fisherfolk, indigenous people etc from around the globe.

But there is another way in which food and ecology feed the growing need for community. Despite the dark cynicism of the 'we're all in it together' claim made by the current UK Coalition Government and the 'Bullingdon Club Cabinet', ecological crises bring common needs into sharp focus. William Ophuls, in his classic text *Ecology and the Politics of Scarcity* (1977) argued that ecological crises make the individualistic basis of society defined around 'inalienable rights, the purely self-defined pursuit of happiness' and 'liberty as maximum freedom of action' at best problematic. Indeed he also argued if resources become more scarce then much of our liberal political philosophy would disappear and we would inhabit a Hobbesian world, where life is 'nasty, brutish and short'.

Ophul's call to action was over thirty years ago and yet little has changed. Indeed things might even be worse given that we now have hyper consumerism and its evil twin 'productivism' – making things we don't need then creating agencies to persuade ourselves to buy them.

As Professor Phil Hanlon and Sandra Carlisle point out in *AfterNow*, the opening book in this series, there's an incredible irony at the heart of the current system:

> With our identities largely constructed around consumption, the economic system exploits the very crisis that it creates by proffering its various goods as solution. [51]

Our response must be to regain some autonomy and independence of mind. We need to become critical thinkers and there is no better avenue than food and health to shock us into creative action

Land and people

> Somewhere is better than anywhere.
> Flannery O Connor

Scottish community food projects of the type described above are leading the way, but behind them we have a real problem with land-ownership and democracy. This is a problem in most countries but is particularly acute in Scotland. We are faced with a fundamental disconnect between land and people. We often don't know who owns the land. We don't know what's grown on it and we don't have any concept that collectively we could benefit from it. This isn't true in many comparable European countries.

As Andy Wightman documents so powerfully in his books on land ownership in Scotland, for centuries Scotland has had disastrously concentrated patterns of land ownership. For example, currently in a country of 19 million acres and five million people, a mere 1252 landowners (0.025% of the population) own two-thirds of the privately owned rural land. This land ownership is so carefully protected and defended, and its inhabitants so harshly treated over the centuries that it remains a potent political issue. [52]

The consequence of divorce from land and food is, inevitably, divorce from nature. This quickly becomes inter-generational knowledge loss and alienation. At a certain point nobody cares because the object or focus has gone. Care about what?

Carolyn Steel author of *The Hungry City* has charted how the relationship between land and people altered fundament-ally since canning technology and the growth of the railways. These technological changes have accelerated vastly in recent years. Steel writes:

> Today, the fact that most of us buy our food from supermarkets has changed the way we inhabit cities fundamentally. Instead of heading into town to buy food, we drive out to large, anonymous boxes. The civic aspect of food selling has disappeared, and along with it, much of the character and purpose of our town centres. The latest trend is for large supermarkets like Tesco to become urban developers, offering local councils incentives to allow them to build large chunks of city with mega-stores at their core – effectively creating captive markets for their business. [53]

But as we've seen, this state of affairs is now being challenged. More and more communities are finding ways to create lasting alternatives. These initiatives in Aberdeen, East Kilbride, Edinburgh and Glasgow are just a handful of examples of efforts to reconnect and restore. They may be small in scale but they have the potential to be scaled-up and to have a huge impact because the tools they bring to people's hands are ones that will be with them forever.

If these projects seem small they also have a core resilience which is in marked contrast to the current system. The fuel protests of 2000 blockaded fuel refineries and oil depots. It exposed the crucial weakness in the food chain of the 'just in time' delivery principles of the big retailers. Panic buying of petrol was inevitable and the country quickly ground to a halt.

When people have virtually no alternatives to the super-markets, few skills, little land, and very few alternative supplies, inevitably there is a lack of any diversity in the shopping landscape. It is brittle, one-dimensional and totally reliant on one point of sale. Without fuel to drive our cars to the market, and without trucks to deliver goods daily to these vast stores, we are, as has been suggested 'nine meals from anarchy'. [54]

In 2011 a number of us launched **Blasda,** Scotland's local food feast. Blasda is Gaelic for tasty, delicious, appetising, sweet. We wanted to use a Gaelic word to call attention to the cultural revival that's taking place in Scotland. There is, if not actual pride, at least less cultural self-hatred going on. After years of dogged 'inferiorism', this is a start.

So we started from the idea of 'taste' and argued that food should taste of something, and be connected to a place. In some respects we were echoing the thinker Mitchell Davis who asked the provocative question, 'What does a better food system taste like?' [55]

Davis has argued that if our food system was designed for taste, processed foods and barely ripe tomatoes would be the exception, not the norm. Taste, Davis says, is a powerful tool for social change. We agree. So Blasda kicked off asking people to come forward and create a local food feast that celebrated the taste of their region, their town, their place.

We created a map and started charting the responses as communities began to plan and host their own celebrations.

In the Borders **Moffatcan** hosted a huge ceilidh and showed off their unique aquaponics system where sustainable fish are reared in an ingenious closed-loop system. It is a brilliant example of how the food revolt is rarely about a return to the past. It's about innovation and fresh thinking while refusing to discard the best from traditional methods.

In Uist over 800 people gathered to learn about their own seafood and cheese-making, watch chef demonstrations and take part in hands-on cooking workshops.

In Glasgow a huge local food feast at the Briggait brought people together from across the city. In 2011 and 2012 events also took place in Dunbar, Dysart, Inverness, Aberdeen, Eigg, Muck and places in between. In Leith and Claggan and the Gairloch and other places too numerous to mention, something was happening.

'We need to re-invent a food culture for all that is based on place, is attuned to seasonality and that people have some control over.'

CHAPTER SIX

Scottish perspectives

How can we take all this disparate activity and claim that it's meaningful, connected? And isn't there a contradiction in claiming that we are in the midst of a 'food revolution' when the vast majority of people still source their food via one of the big retailers? [56]

However, what is evidently clear is that the system is at breaking point and new ideas and practices are emerging. We know that 63% of people surveyed by the Scottish Agricultural College in 2011 wanted more access to local food. Nowhere near that number can get it. As demand far outstrips supply wholesale change must be coming.

Prior to the smoking ban which came into force in Scotland in March 2006 just about everyone said that we couldn't possibly stop people smoking in pubs. Less than a decade on and it seems unimaginable that people were ever prepared to frequent smoke-filled pubs. Eating local food could well be similar. We may quickly move to the situation where the very idea of transporting food around the planet, out of season, will seem as ridiculous as folk lighting up in restaurants, trains or planes.

A vitally important question is what part the food movement

can play in reducing the massive assault on our ecosystems and habitats that we are increasingly aware of. How can the food movement help create community and antidote the rampant individualism of our age? What role can we play in offering simple healthy food to people who are overfed and undernourished? And crucially, how can we make a substantial, and quick, contribution to the transformation to a low carbon society given that we are currently teetering on the brink of runaway climate change?

We need to re-invent a food culture for all that is based on place, is attuned to seasonality and that people have some control over. But what's the specifically Scottish context for this? For reasons that I set out below, I passionately believe that we are uniquely placed to bring some important insights to these challenges. In this chapter I want to talk about place, thrift, generalism, and common sense.

Why place matters

Place matters for one simple reason – if we have no connection we don't care. And if we don't care we will sit back and do nothing to stop the damaging abuse and exploitation of the natural world.

One consequence from an almost total dislocation from place is that we don't know where we come from and we often don't know where we are. Given this we certainly can't hope to know where we are going.

It is now commonplace to complain that children don't understand where their food comes from. But the truth is that this type of disconnect is a much more widespread phenomenon. Essential goods just appear in shops . . . clothes for £4 . . . a chicken for £2.50 . . . then we act shocked when a 'documentary' 'uncovers' that lo and behold someone somewhere is being exploited, in a village far, far away to produce these items for us.

However, thanks to our information age this formerly undisclosed world is now becoming more and more transparent. Reality is leaching to the surface.

One of the positive aspects of consuming from the region in which we live is that everything becomes more knowable as local areas can be understood, mapped, walked and in this sense controlled by the communities they serve. A regional scale allows for vernacular knowledge to be applied. Indeed I see this as a fundamental part of 'the democratic intellect', and a potentially crucial part of a participatory democracy.

Scale is also critical if we are thinking about ownership. In the past 'public ownership' meant state control of large industries. But public ownership takes on a different meaning when we are talking about a scale that is regionally defined (or even closer to home). This type of public ownership would not be remote and bureaucratic.

So place needs to be reclaimed and re-understood by mapping our foodsheds and by understanding what our city-region can appropriately produce. To help us here we have the ground-breaking writing of the great Scottish thinker, Patrick Geddes (1854-1932). Geddes was a pioneer of town planning and, since his work received worldwide recognition, he was hugely influential. His work in Scotland, France, the Near East and India on the principle of 'Place-Work-Folk' remains relevant to contemporary issues of sustainable development, regionalism and locality, economic and community regeneration, environmental quality and social inclusion. The American intellectual Lewis Mumford was a disciple of Geddes and he devised a theory of planning and regional design. This work too can help transform our understanding of the relationship between the city and the region.

But Geddes' work has even more relevance than that to food policy. 'Some people have strange ideas that they live by money. They think energy is generated by the circulation of coins.' That oft quoted thought comes from Geddes' final lecture at University College Dundee in 1918, but while it is apt it is important to see it within context. Geddes said:

> How many people think twice about a leaf? Yet the leaf is the chief product and phenomenon of Life: this is a green world, with animals comparatively few and small, and all dependent upon the leaves. By leaves we live. Some people have strange ideas that they live by money. They think energy is generated by the circulation of coins. But the world is mainly a vast leaf-colony, growing on and forming a leafy soil, not a mere mineral mass: and we live not by the jingling of our coins, but by the fullness of our harvests.

He was later to add more succinctly, on a tour of California: 'Sheep eat grass'.

So Geddes provides us with not only a regional theory of planning but also a conception of ecology that demands that we give priority to basic facts of nature. These have been ignored as we have allowed profiteers to dictate and dominate how and what we eat. Feeding diseased cattle brain to ruminants was the cause of BSE. It may well have been a profitable notion but in ignoring Geddes' basic precepts we endangered and undermined our agriculture system as well as human health.

Within the notion of 'place' there are several more specific and useful categories that should be applied: *scale, proximity, intimacy, and immediacy*.

Very few people in policy or politics talk about *scale* any more. It's now a given that scale and aspiration are global. Indeed the ultimate goal for any business and the solitary measure of its success is export/import – i.e. to 'go global'. So radically re-localised urban food systems will need a different set of standards and a different set of aspirations. A food project has to be deemed successful if its food tastes really good, if it has aesthetic qualities, if its freshness and cleanliness are excellent, and if it's innovative and friendly.

Proximity needs to be reconceptualised – food miles are not just about carbon, they also hinder the development of a sustainable local economy and the knock-on effects this brings. Local food does not mean 'Scottish' or 'UK'. Only a regional framework can help people re-think distance. In a world where we are encouraged to always think in terms of 'the global', it's telling that the Scottish Government's new 'food hub' is titled 'Sourcing for Growth'. Redefining the proximity of our food system must involve rethinking growth, otherwise we perpetuate the problem by assuming that all and every food business should aim solely for growth and ultimately export growth.

We are never going to 'unglobalise' food. But we might restore enough knowledge and diversity to allow a local food movement to fulfil its potential. This is part culture-knowledge (creating enough demand from people who care about their food) and part infrastructure-conditions to allow this to happen. These elements combine, so that, for example, if there is an abattoir on the island of Mull, it helps local farmers, butchers, retailers and restaurants promote their local produce.

We also need to make our new approach to food involve the notion of *intimacy*. It is best to think of this as the opposite of detached and invisible. Currently we have a 'bowling alone' approach to food. Not only is such food detached and untraceable but people often buy processed ready-meals because they will be eaten in isolation. Re-imagining ways in which people can come together and have a less alienating food experience is essential.

Immediacy needs to be re-thought. We have Attention Deficit Hyperactivity Disorder about food. This can be seen not just in our impulsive jumping from one food trend to the next, but also our wolfing food at our desks, while walking down the street or in front of our TVs. Each Christmas you can witness panic-buying as people 'stock up' their fridges and freezers to groaning excess despite the fact that most shops barely shut over the holiday period these days. Indeed it must be folk-memory and a deep insecurity about 'having enough' that creates such extraordinary panic buying. The tragedy is that so much of it is later thrown away.

Food needs time to grow or be reared. It needs time to be picked or shopped for and it needs time to be cooked. Most crucially it needs time to eat. Food immediacy in Scottish cities could mean neighbourhood market gardens, instead of weekly farmers markets. It means more frequent shopping in local stores rather than a big weekly shop in a supermarket.

Different models of production

Faced with the challenges of climate change, food security, and environmental degradation, we should be clear and coherent about the model of development we want for our food system in Scotland.

We could term the current way of doing things the 'disconnection model'. It is highly centralised and dominated by large processing, trading and retail companies and is highly dependent on global trade and markets. This model is characterised by the increasing disconnection between how food is produced and consumed, and disconnected from local ecosystems and regional societies.

Instead of our grotesquely centralised approach we need to adopt what we could call the 'connection model'. This is much more attractive as it is more autonomous and less commodified. It is based on the ecological capital of farming, the reproduction of short and decentralised supply chains and on building links between consumers and producers.

'Place' isn't the only yardstick we can use to define its success. We should also take a wider view and re-think concepts like 'quality' 'efficiency' 'cost' and 'value'. Each has become emptied of real meaning, and one-dimensional. Given our health crisis we must continually ask what are the true costs of food without nourishment?

The environmental crisis we are facing will mean that we all will know more about our geography, what Geddes called the 'literature of locality'. The good news is the future tastes good.

Scottish thinkers, cultural values, and methodology

Geddes isn't the only Scottish thinker to guide us. What about the work of the great Scottish environmentalist from Dunbar, John Muir? He wrote:

> Most people are on the world, not in it – have no conscious sympathy or relationship to anything about them – undiffused, separate, and rigidly alone like marbles of polished stone, touching but separate. [57]

For Muir this was a comment about our relationship to the natural world, but I'd like to suggest that the idea of being 'on the world but not in it' is as much about social dislocation as it is about ecological failure. In other words, the search for community is the search for ecology. We need to think about eco-communities not eco-systems and we need to think about community re-building as intrinsically tied to working within the limits of an actual existing natural world. This is particularly true as we build towards a time where the need for resilience (economic, social, cultural, ecological, and psychological) will become an essential fact of life and not just an abstract concept. For Geddes, re-situating the individual in the world was the basic condition for changing the course of human evolution and opening up a brighter future.

John Muir's analysis is mirrored by the American farmer

and writer, Wendell Berry, who wrote:

> If we speak of a healthy community we cannot be
> speaking of a community that is only human. We
> are talking about a neighbourhood of humans plus
> the place itself: its soil, its water, its air and all the
> families and tribes of the non-human creatures that
> belong to it . . . if this community is healthy, it is
> likely to be sustainable, largely self-sufficient and
> free of tyranny. This means that it is they and not
> the central government that must control the land,
> the forests, the rivers and the seas, from which
> specific communities derive their sustenance. [58]

At the moment the scale and metric we are using is the 'individual' and the 'globe'. Therefore our task in reconstructing a viable food system is not only about creating a low carbon sustainable way of feeding ourselves (though that is essential). It is not just about creating a food culture that won't kill us (though this seems like a good idea). Nor is it just about reclaiming our food economy from the extractive hands of a few supermarkets. It is primarily about creating a restorative practice so that we have communities, households and at least three moments a day that are about a whole, well-functioning world not a fractured, disconnected and abusive one.

Wendell Berry, once wrote:

> If we want to be at peace, we will have to waste
> less, spend less, use less, need less. The most
> alarming sign of the state of our society now is that
> our leaders have the courage to sacrifice the lives of
> young people in war but not the courage to tell us
> that we must be less greedy and less wasteful. [59]

Throughout this book I have referred to the idea of 'living within limits' and explored the notion of 'enough'. Scotland is a country which still has a strong sense of the importance of the collective and the common good. These can be drawn on to help us move towards a lower carbon food economy.

I passionately believe that we can't and shouldn't aim to connect *individuals* with their urban and geographical space but whole communities, neighbourhoods, city-regions and the wider Scottish nation with its own sense of place. Again I think this approach could really find favour in Scotland as we are less focused on the individual and individual self-expression.

The focus on individualism which dominates so much of Western culture is a toxic legacy of our era as it results in an unhealthy obsession with the self. This is particularly true in the realm of food where discussion and understanding has for a long time been about individuals' tastes and preferences, allergies and dietary obsessions. This has detracted from a broader analysis of what is wrong with the food system and the wider economic system.

We also need to be clear that the local food movement isn't another fad and is very different from what's gone before. Up till now we've had whole foods and slow food, fast food and organics. We've had road food, and freeganism, Masterchef and Naked Chefs, the F Word and Atkins . . . The difference about the local food movement, is – it's not actually about 'YOU' any more. Again this is likely to chime with many Scots who often dislike the self-obsessed aspect of contemporary culture.

Scotland is often derided for its lack of entrepreneurial spirit or its people's lack of confidence. But such dampened aspiration might be a saving grace in the new world we are entering. What's more if we are to enter a steady-state economy then the very poverty we have experienced historically might inform a new outlook. Why waste good resources? Why not make the most of what you've got?

Indeed thrift may be a particularly strong cultural value which we could make use of in Scotland. Roseanna Cunningham MSP was laughed at when, as Environment Minister, she suggested we darn our socks to help save the planet and stop being a throwaway society. But she was on to something and I can't imagine a current Westminster minister making such a suggestion. Perhaps the idea of a thrift economy can have some traction in Scotland as it is such a strong part of Scotland's tradition. Ours is a culinary tradition of thrift and innovation and sweet delights to brighten the cold winters – the Scotch Broth that uses a shank to produce rich flavour and feed a family for £1.

If we can have increased access to the land and a restored pride in our produce and our capabilities, then a more resilient food culture could thrive – one that sees worth in broth and values the amazing properties of kale. Under this new sensibility the black humour of Irn-Bru, Scotland's 'other national drink' and the deep fried Mars bar could be replaced by celebrating the superfoods of oats, raspberries and other native foods.

A generalist approach to food policy

I believe that currently we have too much industry control of our food. Our vernacular knowledge is often ignored. What we need is transparency and the space to come up with entirely fresh ways of approaching food policy and growing as well as health and well-being.

So what is this generalism and how can it help democratise food policy? It's a philosophical approach akin to holism that has been described as the bedrock of Scottish education for centuries. It was laid out by the philosopher George Davie in his celebrated work *The Democratic Intellect* (1961). It encapsulates the thinking style and practice of the likes of Hugh MacDiarmid and Patrick Geddes. Geddes describes it thus:

> [a] general and educational point of view must be brought to bear on every specialism. The teacher's outlook should include all viewpoints. . . Hence we must cease to think merely in terms of separated departments and faculties and must relate these in the living mind; in the social mind as well – indeed, this above all. [60]

In 2009 the Scottish Government published its very first 'cross-cutting' food policy. [61] It had a huge impact on what people were trying to do and had real scope and ambition to it in as much as it's attempting to reconcile and combine issues around health, sustainability, 'prosperity' and 'secure and resilient food systems'.

But it also suffered from being a jumble of competing elements rather than a synthesis. The reality is that it's very difficult to achieve a food policy that is: 'wealthier & fairer, smarter, healthier, safer & stronger, and greener' without addressing the relationship and tensions between these objectives.

If we can draw on our generalist tradition we may be able to disentangle some of those competing narratives and progress from the notion 'cross-cutting' to a practice that genuinely reflects the common good.

The *National Food and Drink Policy: Recipe for Success* was a landmark in Scottish policy, as it recognised for the first time the importance of the food system as a whole, and did not treat it as an issue that was subsidiary to the economy and health. Its authors have to be congratulated for this positive development. However, if this policy is to mean anything, it needs to let people, particularly non-professionals, take charge of the process and allow creative dynamism. What's more, this area of policy remains industry-dominated and represents the priorities and values of those industries, namely farming, the meat industry, the supermarkets and industrial-scale fishing. Let's look at these points in more detail.

The Scottish food and drinks policy was developed with the help of the 'Leadership Forum', a group of high-profile individuals and experts charged with responsibility to make recommendations on issues related to health, environment, affordability and the economy.

The Scottish Government also consulted the public in developing *Recipe for Success* and found that their top three priorities are diet and nutrition (68%), local food and local economies (49%) and health promotion (44%). However, as presently conceived, the *National Food and Drink Policy* favours the industry's agenda. Thus it is 'export growth' which is promoted and not local food economies and health. The Scottish Government wants to see the contribution of food and drink to the national economy raised to £10 billion by 2017 but this economic goal alone will not assure sustainable food consumption and production for Scotland.

What's more the basis for this target figure for food industry growth is not clear, nor is the impact of achieving this target on domestic production, diet, land use and greenhouse gas emissions.

There is also no continuing public forum for discussing the implementation or reporting progress. However, the Scottish Government recognises the need for 'food advocacy' and has convened a group of stakeholders to discuss how this should be taken forward. From the discussions, the most desirable option seems to be to create 'a Memorandum of Understanding' or 'Charter for Food Advocacy'. This would involve a loose group of NGOs, academics and others who ascribe to coordinated messages and actions. There is no strong view as yet if this should be initiated by government itself, or if the current Scottish Government should approach an existing organisation to take this idea forward.

Governments and their political will can be transient, depending on the economic and social context. But the level of change now required makes the creation of a robust and critical Food Leadership Team (FLT) or similar advocacy group necessary. This would then ensure that the gains of the current food policy are not lost and that ideas will be contributed to an evolving food policy.

A new Food Leadership Team should be independent of government and cross-sectoral, with a fair representation of all the interest groups and stakeholders, from private business to campaigning NGOs, food poverty groups, schools, hospitals, community organisations, academics, experts, farmers, thinkers, youth groups, women's organisations, public officials and wider networks. The FLT could act both as a monitoring body of the *National Food and Drink Policy* and also as a hub of joined-up thinking, incorporating creative proposals, developing new indicators, and mobilising action.

The FLT would create meaningful connections between disparate food interests in Scotland. It would also link with movements and groups internationally, making sure the way we consume and produce food in Scotland has the minimum social and environmental impacts on other countries, and work together with them for a more sustainable and democratic food system worldwide.

Up till now the Scottish Parliament has had very limited involvement in food policy. But this could change. To avoid the FLT becoming a 'talking shop', and to redress the power imbalance in the global food system, the proposals approved by the FLT should have a direct connection with MSPs. The FLT could provide a credible and recognisable arena to apply pressure as a focused critical mass – a space where a new food democracy might emerge.

As argued above, a Food Leadership Team would have to be drawn from a much wider representative group than business and industry. It should ideally include people from all walks of life. A generalist approach would enable this group to draw on expertise from a range of specialisms and then take a considered view. In short, a generalist approach would begin to democratise the whole process.

Common sense

For some readers this may seem like an overly theoretical proposal. But a generalist approach could be a tool to bring common sense back to policy and public thinking. It could be a mechanism to help us stand back and look at why we have the current obsession with economic growth and whether it is sustainable. It will help us draw on expertise without being beholden to experts, or top-down thinking which has repeatedly failed to help us deal with this issue.

Common sense notions might suggest other measurements of 'success' in food. Other 'metrics' might include:

- The uptake and quality of our school meals and the health of our children

- The number of new farmers taking on land

- The quality of our soil

- The diversity of our seed stock

- The intake of vitamins and nutrients

- The quality of our animal husbandry

- The levels of real innovation in what we grow

- The taste of our produce.

Just as Gross Domestic Product is now widely derided as a crude, one-dimensional measure of economic health, it won't take much for people to see that 'growth' is never going to be an adequate measurement for our food system.

We need to create forums and platforms where ordinary people have some control over the food system that has failed us.

Time is the often the enemy of participation as people live busy and often stressful lives. We could consider restructuring the working week so that people have space to take part, to consider, to slow-cook, to grow. Fridays could become food day in a new four day week in Scotland, where people can tend their allotment, prepare a special meal, and shop carefully.

Many studies have shown that productivity actually increases if people work shorter hours, and more recently we have seen the explosion of work hours outside office hours as people 'log on' and check emails throughout the evenings. A four day week would probably just be a rebalancing of actual hours spent in any given week, a gesture towards better quality family life, reduced stress and perhaps even the option for us to create a more fulfilling and creative food culture.

Balancing tradition and change

> *Lean gu dluth ri cliu do shinnsre,'* says the Gaelic proverb: Let us follow in the brave path of our ancestors.
>
> F.M. McNeill

The Gaelic proverb isn't a call for a return to the past. It's a suggestion that we disregard our traditions at our peril. Part of the disconnect we have between place and people is a loss of traditional skills and knowledge, and some of this is likely to be essential in the years ahead as we lessen our dependence on technology, de-industrialise aspects of our society and re-tune to natural cycles.

We are living through a revival in Scottish culture and this has included fresh thinking about what to eat and grow. Access to our own food heritage will provide essential tools but more importantly will encourage us to value plants and foodstuffs that do well here.

The balance between old and new is complex. There's been talk recently in Scotland about the need for a 're-industrial revolution'. Supporters of the Green Party or environmental movement, may argue for a de-industrial revolution, but the truth is that we can choose where and when to apply technologies. I want an industrial railway system and tidal energy system, but I don't want an industrial pie. I may choose to crowd-source my oat harvest on Twitter, to use CarrotMob to shift food purchases or to use new technologies for updates on what producers will be at the farmers market.

CHAPTER SEVEN

Scotland's local food revolution

> Going local does not mean walling off the outside
> world. It means nurturing local businesses which
> use local resources sustainably, employ local
> workers at decent wages, and serve primarily local
> consumers. It means becoming more self-sufficient,
> and less dependent on imports. Control moves
> from the boardrooms of distant corporations, and
> back to the community, where it belongs.
>
> Michael Shuman, *Going Local*

As we've seen repeatedly in this book there are many communities and individuals who are now doing things differently. I now want to describe some of the people who are leading the change in this direction. They are an unlikely collection of pioneers and innovators who are no doubt inspired by different experiences and beliefs.

In October 2009 a coalition of people came together in Dunbar to form **Nourish**, a network of organisations committed to a more sustainable Scottish food system. The event was organised by One Planet Food, Sustaining Dunbar, the Soil Association Scotland and Transition Scotland Support.

After a weekend of sharing the best (and worst) of food experiences and exploring regional variations the group agreed on a declaration which four years on still makes sense. We said:

> We are working towards a sustainable Scotland in which, in every region **we produce more of what we eat and eat more of what we produce**.
>
> We believe a more localised food system would be better for the environment, health, community and economy of our country. We are building a movement to create a food system that is:
>
> • Locally based with shorter supply chains
> • Promotes and respects seasonality
> • Resilient
> • Fair and accessible to all
> • Creates and maintains a sustainable livelihood for producers
>
> These steps are essential in order to ensure a fairer more equitable food system appropriate for a low carbon economy. [62]

It's worth focusing on a number of people involved in this network as they are the key drivers in the work that has started to transform Scottish food. This is by no means an exhaustive list. They are simply individuals and projects which represent a far wider movement of change.

Cafés and restaurants

Examples of cafés and restaurants involved in this movement are appearing everywhere and not just in urban centres. For example, the **Real Food Café** in Tyndrum has been pioneering locally sourced foods and has been hugely successful in offering an alternative to the usual drivers' pitstop. **Eusk** in

Oban has been celebrating and reviving quality sustainable seafood cooking. In Edinburgh cafés like the **Larder** and new restaurants like the **Gardener's Cottage** and **Timberyard** have committed themselves to seasonality in a way no other restaurants have done until now. A glance at Timberyard's February menu lists simple seasonal dishes: 'oak smoked sirloin, January king cabbage, ramson, carrot, onion' with a pudding of 'sea buckthorn posset, rhubarb'.

These dishes also point to the influence of the revival in foraging and wild food that has taken hold recently as people strive to unearth old knowledge and reconnect with seasons and rhythms. The restaurant has its own smokery, filters and carbonates its own water and has its own raised beds.

These are all outstanding examples of the new wave of Scottish cooking and they are at the heart of the local food revolution. While there are dozens of examples at the upmarket end of the spectrum (Neil Forbes's **Café St Honoré**, in Edinburgh, **Tom Kitchin**, **Andrew Fairlie**) what's really exciting is the emergence of a range of mainstream, affordable cafés and delis where localism, organics and seasonality are becoming the new norm. Suzanne O'Connor and Carina Contini at the **Scottish Café and Restaurant**; **Iglu**; the **Airds Hotel and Restaurant** at Port Appin in Argyll; the **Mains of Scotstown Inn** in Bridge of Don, Aberdeenshire; and **Gamba** (Glasgow) are all part of the growing list.

Monachyle Mhor is a restaurant and hotel in Scotland's first National Park, overlooking Loch Voil and Loch Doine. They've developed a range of 'Mhor' branded food outlets in and around Callander in the Trossachs. Run by Rob and Jean Lewis the Mhor range in Callander includes a bakery using handmade, preservative-free traditional breads. But it's their fish café and fishmonger that's made an impact. The menu, as well as offering traditional fish suppers, lets you opt for a gastronomic seafood experience: you can select your fish from the counter and ask for it to be grilled, seared, baked or fried.

MHOR Fish won 'Best Newcomer' in the prestigious Observer Food Monthly awards. The review read: 'The accidental chippie. How a very ordinary greasy spoon in a sleepy Perthshire town became the country's finest fish-and-chip shop, the peerless Mhorfish – complete with sparkling water in the batter and beef dripping in the deep-fat fryer.

It is more than a fish and chip shop, however, as the judges recognised: 'it is an aspiring model for what could be a new wave of democratically priced, sustainable fish enterprises.'

Suddenly, intelligent, knowledgeable food people are appearing everywhere. These aren't just producers or business-people. Mark Williams has established a creative niche in Galloway with wild food courses that simply couldn't have existed five years ago.

Phoebe Weller has recently gained a profile for herself as an expert describing, exploring and celebrating Scottish cheese. For a country inured to digesting amorphous lumps of bright orange stuff, the idea of someone exploring the *terroir*, taste and sense of cheese with real depth and sophistication is a revelation in itself. Phoebe does this with wit and charm which may help explain why her cheese-tasting sessions are packed out. It is also is a sign that we are witnessing a renaissance in our food culture.

A driver of change here is that the supermarket system

undermines dairy farming. This forces more and more dairies to innovate, diversify and find new niche products rather than play the game the giant retailers require. In this sense the system's acute dysfunctionality will be part of its ultimate downfall.

Producers

In production, Dave and Wilma Finlay at the **Cream O' Galloway** dairy farm are rewriting the rulebook on good practice in dairy and ethical animal husbandry. On Gigha sustainable organic halibut have become an alternative to the disastrous industrial farmed salmon that blight almost every sea loch in the country. And hand-caught **Isle of Mull Scallops** have led the way in creating sustainable seafood. If there's an added cost for these products, it's a price worth paying as it allows the consumer to sidestep dredged seafood, lice-infested salmon and heavy polluting dairy.

What is becoming more and more evident is the virtuous circle of emerging local markets and innovative or new farmers wanting to try new products or techniques and thus adding value.

Chillilicious is a great example of a crazy idea that few would have expected to work but it is thanks to the way it is being driven forward with ingenuity and passion. There's no history of growing chillis in Fife – why should there be? But with the right varieties and conditions they can do very well, and provide a welcome contribution to the Fife larder – Chillilicious is Scotland's first and only chilli farm, making them the most northerly chilli producer in the UK. Run by

Patricia and Stacey Galfskiy, they produce delicious chilli food products. It's precisely the sort of viable innovation that's needed to bring diversity (and heat) to the Scottish local food market.

Writers and activists

In the past we've spent a lot of time being told, and telling ourselves, that our culture is second rate and our food is, if anything, third rate. We almost revel in our self-image as the boozy, self-destructive fat man of Europe. It's a form of swaggering nihilism. It's a great incentive to say 'Wha's Like Us?' and do nothing. Part of the problem facing Scots has been a dearth of knowledge about our own culinary history. What traditions do you look to beyond the terminally couthy or the tartan-tainted faux highland tourist cliché? Until recently, we have not been well served by Scottish food writers and publishers. For decades we have seen our cooking dreadfully misrepresented by tomes adorned with tartan tablecloths, pheasants, cock a leekie and cranachan.

Murdo Macdonald has described how parts of Scottish culture have been obscured, lost, marginalised. His interest has been the visual arts but his ideas can also be applied to our food heritage. It's a 'mislaid history' one lost not out of some great conspiracy but just because it's been 'deemed unimportant'. Part of the recovery is to excavate elements of food history and examine it in a new light.

A few individuals have now made great headway in different areas – community growing, food writing, health and well-being research, soil improvement – and represent a deeper and growing understanding.

Catherine Brown's *Scottish Seafood: its History and Cooking* (2011) was a breakthrough. She draws on traditional Scottish seafood recipes, from Cullen skink to partan bree, Solway scallops and bacon to Musselburgh steak and oyster pie and in the process creates a long overdue overview of Scottish cuisine. In her pages we find a wonderful but forgotten account of how our ancestors gathered and cooked seafood, be it seaweeds like carrageen, dulse and tangle, shellfish like limpets, mussels, razor-shell clams, crabs and lobsters, or a whole range of fish species. In her previous book *Broths to Bannocks: a history of cooking in Scotland from 1690 to the present day* (1990) Brown investigated the roots of national cuisine from a study of archive material and historical cookery books. It's a start and an important one.

Joanna Blythman has made a very different but also crucially important contribution to our understanding. In the *The Food We Eat* (1998), *Shopped* (2004), *Bad Food Britain* (2006) and more recently *What to Eat?* (2012) her rigorous analysis and formidable knowledge have helped shape and articulate the new food understanding that's emerging and coming to the fore. Her writing is relentless, clear and brave. She also eschews orthodoxy and is continually prepared to confront injustices.

In *Scots Cooking* (2000), *Scottish Kitchen* (2003), and *A Cook's Tour of Scotland* (2006), Sue Lawrence began to explore a contemporary version of Scottish cooking and in *The Good Scots Diet* (2013) Maisie Steven dissects the process by which we have lost heritage and nutrients in a post-industrial diet.

These are fragments, but taken collectively – and set alongside the grow-it-yourself movement they are a formidable combination and testimony to a rising sea change in attitudes to food in Scotland.

Growers like Ron Gilchrist who have pioneered high quality composting and soil restoration techniques have been a massive influence on the revival of community growing in the last ten years. Ron has taught a whole generation of people techniques and approaches that have helped develop a grounded community-focused practice, often in some of Scotland's most deprived communities.

Recent writings like Ken Cox's *Fruit and Vegetables for Scotland: What to grow and how to grow it* (2011) document the most suitable varieties for growing here whilst *Flora Celtica – Plants and People in Scotland* by William Milliken and Sam Bridgewater (2004) document the continuously evolving relationship between the Scots and their environment. These have made a significant contribution particularly to the work in community gardens across Scotland, most notably in Glasgow in projects like Urban Roots, Dennistoun Diggers and the Concrete Garden, as well as across the SAGE network.

Working in the Southside of Glasgow for the Hidden Gardens and a series of innovative projects Clem Sandison initiated a Culture Kitchen Relay in 2012 touring the country and sharing and swapping recipes between communities and cooks.

This is a disparate group, and, it could be argued that some of the businesses are just commercial operations. Why should we reckon that profit-making companies are the weather-vane of social change? On their own, these fine initiatives aren't enough. The problem isn't just an impoverished food culture, a sense of inferiorism. The 'solution' isn't just different forms of consumerism, but challenging consumerism itself.

It's a subject explored at length by Phil Hanlon who's After Now project has developed a sustained and nuanced analysis of consumer culture. He criticises the 'obesogenic society' and the deep-rooted problems of contemporary hyper-consumerism, but adds with some optimism:

> Since consumerism as we now see it only emerged during the mid-twentieth century, it's clear that there is no inherent impulse for consumerism in human nature. It was created to serve the needs of Western economies; consumerism emerged as the result of social engineering. Consumerism not only serves capitalism but also helps meet the (sometimes perverse) needs that capitalism creates – needs which are profoundly antithetical to human well-being. [63]

So can this resurgence in interest in and respect for Scottish produce be translated into a more radical change in our food habits that forms part of a rejection of the disposable culture of hyper-consumerism? Only if the local food movement is part of a wider movement for social change and wedded to a shift in values.

Can we, in regaining a sense of value in our regional and seasonal growing capacity, re-connect with nature enough to establish a new outlook based on reverence, thrift and creativity?

Reflecting on the breathtakingly successful urban agriculture programme in Havana, Cuba – now producing more than four million tons a year of the city's food – the architects of this transformation have stated that the essential ingredients were 'necessity, possibility and will'. [64]

We have the necessity, and endless possibility, the test for us in Scotland will be, do we have the will?

Scotland has world leading ambitious climate change targets and our first ever national Food and Drink policy. But the two seem completely separate.

We know that the refrigeration chain constitutes about 15% of the CO_2 emissions from our food yet we celebrate every time a new out-of-town shopping development is announced or a multiple opens a new superstore. We know that greenhouse gas from our agricultural sector has been flat-lining since 2007 – yet we have no coherent plan for reducing this. We know that the way we produce, distribute and consume our food creates 31% of our annual CO_2 each year yet we have no co-ordinated plan for changing this.

We need a specific annual food emissions reduction target and the promotion of low carbon foods as a key goal, aim and indicator. We need a coherent framework for reduction of greenhouse gas emissions from our primary agriculture sector. None of this will be possible simply as policy. It needs to be understood and engaged with throughout society so that people can be part of the change process, not have it handed down to them. But for that to be possible we need some huge institutional shifts to take place that enable participation.

Ultimately good food is about good democracy, so that people can make choices and have influence over their own lives.

Much of this will be dismissed by certian vested interests as utopian or fanciful. But we live in rapidly changing times where the old models of working, and trusted institutions have been proven untrustworthy. The challenge for us with the way we feed ourselves is to create new institutions and new ways of working before the system collapses further in on itself. We need new ground and new tools. Let's get digging.

CHAPTER EIGHT

What you can do

In the introduction to this book I argued that to address our dysfunctional food system we need to change our priorities and the way we eat. Of course, governments must make policy changes – restricting the growth of supermarkets and improving food regulation, for example – but dramatic change will only happen when we begin to act directly and collectively and our actions are rooted in community. Here are a few ideas to help you get started:

Eat more locally and seasonally

- Go to your local farmers' market
- Sign up for a veg box scheme
- Use local shops such as butchers and fishmongers as they are more likely to sell local produce
- Do some research to find out what produce, such as cheese or cereal, is produced or grown near you and where you can buy it
- Pick your own fruit locally when it is available
- Bottle, preserve and pickle fruit and vegetables when they are in season
- If it's too daunting to eat 80% local food and 20% from further afield then simply try to shift the balance more towards food grown in your bioregion. This is still really worthwhile.

Eat less meat

- Reduce portion sizes
- Eat better quality meat or game

- Experiment with vegetarian cookery
- Try to get out of the idea that you should be eating meat with every meal or every day of the week.

Eat more organic produce
- But favour local non-organic produce over organic produce from miles away.

Reduce food waste
- Shop more often buying what you need immediately and don't do a 'big shop' as this often results in food being thrown away
- Always use up left-overs
- Don't always go by sell-by dates as food is often ok to eat even though the date has passed.

Compost more
- Start your own compost heap
- Put food waste in the caddy supplied by your local council.

Processed food
- Try to avoid this as much as possible particularly meat products and ready meals.

Avoid supermarkets
- If there are plans to build or extend a supermarket in your area take part in a campaign against it.

Grow or produce some of what you eat yourself
- This can be a few herbs or salad greens on windowsills, using your garden more for crops and less for ornamental plants or acquiring an allotment
- Get a few chickens to supply your family with eggs
- Bake more, make your own yogurt, beer etc.

Participate in groups and projects about local food
- This can simply be a support or discussion group for people interested in eating more locally
- If no group is available start your own
- If none exists start a group to campaign for allotments in your area or a community orchard or herb garden.
- Frequent cafés and restaurants where the accent is on local/ seasonal food.

Together these actions can half our CO_2 emissions from food and have other benefits such as boosting the local economy, enhancing biodiversity, improving soil conditions and improving health through increased intake of fresh unprocessed foods.

To help you with some of these actions we have some additional resources available on the Scotland's Local Food Revolution section of the website dedicated to this book series www.postcardsfromscotland.co.uk ☐

References

Blythman, Joanna *What To Eat: Food that's good for your health, pocket and plate*, 2013;
Bad Food Britain: How a Nation Ruined Its Appetite, 2000;
Shopped: The Shocking Power of British Supermarkets, 2004

Bookchin, Murray T*oward an Ecological Society*, 1991

Brown, Catherine *Scottish Seafood: its History and Cooking*, 2011
Broths to Bannocks: a history of cooking in Scotland from 1690 to the present day, 1990

Bové, José and Dufour, François *The World Is Not for Sale: Farmers Against Junk Food*, 2002

Carson, Rachel *Silent Spring*, 1962

Cook, Christopher D *Diet for a Dead Planet*, 2004

Cox, Ken *Fruit and Vegetables for Scotland: What to grow and how to grow it*, 2011

Lappé, Frances Moore *Diet for a Small Planet*, 1991

Lawrence, Felicity *Eat Your Heart Out*, 2008

Lawrence, Sue *Scots Cooking*, 2000
Scottish Kitchen, 2003
A Cook's Tour of Scotland, 2006

Luccarelli, Mark *Lewis Mumford and the Ecological Region,* 1995

McCarrison, Robert *Nutrition and Health,* 1982

McGinnis, Michael Vincent (ed) *Bioregionalism,* 1999

McNeill, F Marian *The Scots Kitchen,* 1974

Milliken, William and Bridgewater, Sam *Flora Celtica – Plants and People in Scotland,* 2004

Norberg-Hodge, Helena *Bringing the Food Economy Home, Local Alternatives to Global Agribusiness,* 2002

Ophuls, William *Ecology and the Politics of Scarcity,* 1977

Pollan, Michael *Food Rules,* 2009

Sennett, Richard *The Craftsman,* 2008

Schlosser, Eric *Fast Food Nation: The Dark Side of the All-American Meal,* 2003

Steven, Masie *The Good Scots Diet,* 2013

Stuart, Tristam *Waste: Uncovering the Global Food Scandal,* 2009

Tokar, Brian *Toward Climate Justice,* 2010

Tudge, Colin *Feeding People is Easy,* 2007

Vidal, John *McLibel, Burger Culture on Trial,* 1997

Notes

To read these notes with hyperlinks to most of the articles and reports listed please go to the Scotland's Local Food Revolution section of www.postcardsfromscotland.co.uk

1. Eric Audsley, et al, *How Low Can We Go? An assessment of greenhouse gas emissions from the UK food system and the scope for reduction by 2050.*
2. George Monbiot, 'The road well travelled', *The Guardian*, 30 October 2007.
3. Moray McLaren, *Understanding the Scots*, Frederick Muller, London, 1956, p. 48.
4. See Martin Hickman, 'Supermarkets shun seasonal British food', *The Independent*, 3 June 2010.
5. See Caroline Lucas, 'Stopping the great food swap' – Relocalising Europe's food supply.' Retrieved from http://www.carolinelucasmep.org.uk/wp-content/uploads/file/Stopping%20the%20great%20food%20swap.pdf
6. WHICH? report Feb 2013.
7. Felicity Lawrence, 'The horsemeat scandal: Could there be much more to come?', *The Guardian*, 8 February 2013.
8. Joanna Blythman, 'Big business is bad news for good food – and horse may be the least of our problems', *The Independent*, 12 February 2013.
9. James Bruges, *The Big Earth Book*, Bristol, 2007.
10. For a summary of Justice Bell's judgement go to: http://www.mcspotlight.org/case/trial/verdict/verdict0_sum.html
11. See *The Guardian*, 13 December 2012.
12. See *The Mail Online*, 4 January 2013.
13. see: http://www.munichre.com/en/media_relations/press_releases/2009/2009_11_26_press_release.aspx
14. See the Scottish Government's *Recipe for Success: Scotland's National Food and Drink Policy*, 2009.
15. This is a quote from a 1993 Scottish Office paper on The Scottish Diet. See http://www.scotland.gov.uk/Topics/Statistics/Browse/Health/TrendDiet
16. Stephen Jardine, 'Success story with a sour after-taste', *The Scotsman*, 3 March 2012.

17. See information published by the Trussell Trust on their website. Go to: http://www.trusselltrust.org

18. See 'Save the children launches campaign to help UK families in poverty', *The Guardian,* 5 September 2012.

19 See 'Horsemeat: EU imports and exports data', *The Guardian* datablog.

20 Joanna Blythman, 'Horsemeat or not, it's all junk', *The Guardian* 16 February 2013.

21. Cate Devine, 'How to avoid being misled by labels', *The Herald*, 16 February 2013.

22. See http://www.food.gov.uk/news-updates/news/2013/mar/scotconsult#.UXfmuL-i2JU

23. Rob Edwards, 'Food protection tests slashed by a third in Scotland', *Sunday Herald,* 17 February 2013.

24. Will Hutton, 'The meat scandal shows all that is rotten about our free marketeers', *The Observer*, 17 February 2013.

25. Matthew Taylor and James Meikle, 'Cuts and deregulation fostered horsemeat scandal, says Labour', *The Guardian*, 18 January 2013.

26. Jay Raynor, 'As the horsemeat scandal shows, thuggish supermarkets are endangering our food supply', *The Observer*, 17 February 2013.

27. Natalie Bennett, 'Horsemeat scandal's origin lies in the heart of our economic model', *The Guardian*, 22 February 2013.

28. See BBC News http://www.bbc.co.uk/news/uk-scotland-glasgow-west-21531663

29. Gemma MacKenzie, 'Lochead launches expert food groups', *Farmers Weekly*, 20 February, 2013.

30. See article on UNEP *Our Nutrient World* report http://www.ceh.ac.uk/news/news_archive/smarter-nutrients-use-health-environment_2014_11.html

31 Fiona Harvey, 'Halve meat consumption, scientists urge rich world', *The Guardian*, 18 February 2013.

32. As above.

33. Speech by Terry Leahy on 26 January 2004, www.tesco.com/corporateinfo

34. SRUC, '2011: An analysis of marketing channels for local food in Scotland'.

35. New Economics Foundation, 'Plugging the Leaks', 2008.

36. See Tescopoly, http://www.tescopoly.org

37. 'Supermarkets "killing" dairy sector', *Scottish Farmer*, 25 October, 2012.

38. As above.

39. Fife Diet Food Manifesto 2012. Retrieved from: http://www.fifediet.co.uk/2012/04/20/fife-diet-food-manifesto-2012/

40. See Fife Diet Manifesto.

41. 'Global Food Waste Not, Want Not', Institute of Mechanical Engineers, 2013.

42. Alison Rowat, 'Wasting food could become a matter of life or death', *The Herald*, 11 January 2013.

43. Tristram Suart, *Waste: Uncovering the global food scandal*, W. W. Norton, New York, 2009, p. 32.

44. *Ghost Town Britain*, New Economics Foundation, 2002.

45. 'M. Jahi Chappell, 'Shattering Myths: Can sustainable agriculture feed the world?, PhD Candidate, University of Michigan Department of Ecology and Evolutionary Biology.

46. See 'Climate Change: how a warming world is a threat to our food supplies', *The Observer*, 13 April 2013.

47. See Robert Frank, *Luxury Fever: Weighing the cost of excess*, Simon and Schuster, New York, 1999 and Oliver James, *Affluenza,* Vermilion, London, 2007.

48. See Third Force News, 10 May 2012.

49. See NVA website http://www.nva.org.uk/past-projects/ sage+sow+and+grow+everywhere+and+glasgow+harvest/

50. See http://www.nyeleni.org/spip.php?article290

51. Phil Hanlon and Sandra Carlisle, *AfterNow: What next for a healthy Scotland,* Argyll Publishing, 2012, p.55.

52. See Andy Wightman, *Scotland: Land and Power*, Luath Press, Edinburgh, 1999 and Andy Wightman, *The Poor had no Lawyers*, Birlinn, Edinburgh, 2010.

53. Carolyn Steel, *The Hungry City: How food shapes our lives*, Vintage, London, 2013.

54. See Andrew Simms, 'Nine Meals from Anarchy', *The Guardian*, 11 January, 2010.

55. See http://www.foodtechconnect.com/2012/02/22/james-beard-mitchell-davis-what-a-better-food-system-tastes-like/

56. Even in Fife where we have 5000 people or so taking part in the Fife Diet, this seems a paltry amount when you consider the population is around 350,000.

57. *John of the Mountains: The unpublished journals of John Muir,* University of Wisconsin Press, 1979, p. 320.

58. Wendell Berry, *Sex, Economy, Freedom and Community: Eight essays,* Pantheon Books, New York, 1992, p. 14.

59. Wendell Berry, p. 92.

60. Final lecture by Patrick Geddes to his Dundee students. For the full text see Amelia Defries, *The Interpreter: Geddes*, 1927, pp. 172-190.

61. *Recipe For Success – Scotland's National Food and Drink'Policy.* Retrieved from http://www.scotland.gov.uk/Publications/2009/06/ 25133322/0

62. See Nourish Scotland's website: http:www.nourishscotland.org.uk

63. Phil Hanlon & Sandra Carlisle, *AfterNow: what next for a healthy Scotland?* Argyll Publishing 2012

64. Sinan Koont, 2009, http://monthlyreview.org/2009/01/01/the-urban-agriculture-of-havana

OTHER TITLES IN THIS SERIES

AfterNow: What next for a healthy Scotland?
Phil Hanlon and Sandra Carlisle

ISBN:978 1 908931005 4 £5.99

The authors of this visionary book look at health in
Scotland and beyond health to the main social,
economic, environmental and cultural challenges
of our times. By setting out the 'challenges of
modernity' and showing how we are living through 'a
change of age', they examine the type of
transformational change required to create a more
resilient and healthy Scotland.

Phil Hanlon is Professor of Public Health at
University of Glasgow, and interested in some of
Scotland's most intractable health problems.

Sandra Carlisle has been involved in numerous
health and policy-related research and evaluation
projects including partnership working for social
inclusion and health inequalities and on the social
determinants of health.

The Great Takeover: How materialism, the media and markets now dominate our lives

Carol Craig

ISBN:978 1 908931061 £5.99

This book describes the dominance of materalist values, the media and business in all our lives and how this is leading to a loss of individual and collective well-being. It looks at many of the big issues of our times – debt, inequality, political apathy, loss of self-esteem, pornography and the rise of celebrity culture. The conclusion is simple and ultimately hopeful – we can change our values and our lives.

Carol Craig is Chief Executive of the Centre for Confidence and Well-being which she established in 2004. She is author of *The Scots' Crisis of Confidence* (2003 and 2011); *Creating Confidence: A handbook for professionals working with young people* (2007); and *The Tears that Made the Clyde: Well-being in Glasgow* (2010).

The New Road: charting Scotland's inspirational communities

Alf Young and Ewan Young

ISBN:978 1 908931078 £5.99

A father and son go on a week long journey round Scotland to see at first hand some of the great environmental, social, employment and regeneration projects which are happening round the country. From Dunbar in the south east of Scotland to Knoydart in the north west they meet people involved in projects which demonstrate new ways of living.

Alf Young writes, broadcasts and comments on a range of issues affecting Scotland and the wider world. He retired in 2009 from the *Herald* where he was responsible for comment and opinion. He writes a Saturday column for the *Scotsman* and is a regular contributor to BBC current affairs programmes. Currently chairman of Riverside Inverclyde and of Social Investment Scotland, he is also an economic adviser to the Scottish Council for Development and Industry.

Ewan Young works as Development Officer for the Ullapool Community Trust. Sustainable living is one of his passions. Holding degreess in Planning and Environmental Sustainability, he lives near Ulapool with his wife, Merlin.